ONE STORY

ENCOUNTERING JESUS THROUGH THE BIBLE

TIM HOWEY, 2022

One Story:
Encountering Jesus Through the Bible

© 2021 Tim Howey
All rights reserved.

ISBN 978-0-578-34591-8

GC Collaborative Publishing
Overland Park, Kansas

Printed in the United States of America

Scripture taken from the New King James Version®. Copyright © 1982 by Thomas Nelson. Used by permission. All rights reserved.

WHY I WROTE THIS BOOK

I started down the path to writing this book because God didn't answer my prayer.

Some of the best new directions from God or new levels of brokenness happen when God tells us no.

When our church prayed and tried to raise funds to build a 1200-seat auditorium, God said no. That's how God guided us back to our original church planting strategy. (We are in a 20-year initiative to train and send 100 church planters and missionaries.)

When Cathy and I prayed and tried to adopt a baby girl from North Carolina, God said no. That's how God brought us to new levels of weakness and dependency on Jesus. (Four months later as I studied 2 Corinthians 2:7, God told me we would have a daughter someday named Mallon. Two and a half years after that, we adopted that girl's half-sister. Her name is Mallon.)

When Paul prayed and tried to keep ministering in Asia on his second missionary journey, God said no twice (Acts 16). That's how God guided him to cross the Aegean Sea and take the gospel to Europe.

When Jesus prayed about avoiding the cross, God said no (Matthew 26). That's how Jesus died on the cross to pay for our sins, reconcile us to God, and give us His life and joy today.

When our church prayed and tried to hire a discipleship pastor in 2010, God said no. That's how I wrote the first OWNit365 Bible reading plan for our church: the Whole Bible Plan. Then I wrote the New Testament Plus plan. Then I wrote the Bible reading plan in this book: the One Story Plan.

I started down this path because God told me no.

I wrote this book for three reasons: (1) To help people see Jesus through the Bible from Genesis to Revelation. (2) To give our church a tool for Bible-reading discipleship groups called "Huddles." (3) To guide our church as we teach through the Bible in a year.

My prayer is that God will use this book to bring the Bible to life for you; that you'll see how the Bible is interconnected; that you'll see Jesus in every story; that you'll grow in believing God loves you; and you'll love Him more than anything.

With love,
Tim

WHAT JESUS SAID ABOUT THE BIBLE

Jesus was Almighty God clothed in human flesh. Jesus proved He was God when He rose again from the dead. What Almighty God in human form said about the Bible matters.

Jesus believed the Bible. He talked about people as if they were real: Noah, Abraham, Isaac, Jacob, Lot, Lot's wife, Jonah, etc. Jesus talked about events as if they happened: the Creation, Adam and Eve's marriage, Abel's murder, Noah's flood, Sodom's destruction, Moses' burning bush, Jonah swallowed, etc. Jesus told the Sadducees that their skepticism revealed they didn't know the power of God to fulfill His word (Matthew 22). Jesus told two disciples on the road to Emmaus that they were foolish not to believe all that the prophets said (Luke 24). Jesus, the God-man, believed the Bible.

Jesus also said the Bible was about Himself. Jesus told the Jews that the Scriptures testify of Him and Moses wrote about Him (John 5). Jesus showed the two disciples on the road to Emmaus how all the prophets in the Hebrew Bible talked about Him (Luke 24). Paul wrote that every Old Testament law and practice pictured Jesus: dietary laws, holiday laws, Sabbath laws (Colossians 2). Jesus, the God-man, said the Bible was about Himself.

The Bible is about a Person. Salvation is about a Person. Life is about a Person. Our message is about a Person: the Person of Christ.

When you read the Bible, you're reading about Jesus. The Bible is One Story: His Story.

HOW I WOULD USE THIS BOOK

I would use this book as I was taught.

I encourage you to experiment with doing that too. That's what Jesus' disciples do. We teach others as we've been taught, so they teach others, so they teach others to the fourth generation spiritually (2 Timothy 2:2).

For Bible reading, I would start by praying that God opens my eyes spiritually then read the passages looking for three things: (1) Historically — What does the Bible say here? (2) Doctrinally — What does this passage teach me about God or the future? Every passage teaches us about Jesus. (3) Personally — What can I apply to my life today? I would try to do six readings a week and not beat myself up when I miss a day. That's Bible reading.

For prayer, once a week I would look back at my calendar, task list, and Bible readings over the last week to make a "thank God list." Then I would look forward on my calendar and task list to record events, decisions, deadlines, or progress needed over the next week to make a prayer list. I would try to pray my "thank God list" and prayer list six times a week and not beat myself up when I miss a day. That's prayer.

My rhythm would hopefully be to pray and read six days a week and reflect and make new lists on the seventh day while not beating myself up when I missed.

My advice to you would be to try this. If it works for you, great. God wired you this way. If it doesn't work for you, great. God wired you a different way. The most important goal for you is to connect with Jesus how you're wired through prayer and Bible reading on a regular basis.

May you continually refresh your mind and heart with His word and love and enjoy Jesus more than anything.

ETERNITY PAST — GOD'S ETERNAL PLAN FROM BEFORE TIME BEGAN

Before the universe existed, before there was such a thing as time, there was just God: only God. God the Father, God the Son, and God the Holy Spirit existed together, uncreated, in a love-filled relationship. Then Jesus, who is the image of the invisible God, created the universe for His own pleasure and purposes. You were created for God's own pleasure and purposes.

1

READING

> *For by Him [Jesus] all things were created that are in heaven and that are on earth, visible and invisible, whether thrones or dominions or principalities or powers. All things were created through Him and for Him. (Colossians 1:16)*

SCRIPTURE READINGS:

- Genesis 1:1-5
- John 1:1-18
- Colossians 1:15-19

Questions? Learnings? Praises? Prayers? To Do's? Jesus is...?

DATE:

2 READING

THE CREATION — GOD CREATES THE UNIVERSE

Jesus, as God the Son, spoke the universe into existence. He said, "Let there be light… space… earth…" Then God the Father, Son, and Spirit all agreed and said, "Let Us make man in Our image." Do you realize every person bears God's image? Today Jesus sits at the right hand of God and is the only true Heir of all things. You are a part of Jesus' inheritance.

And: "You, Lord [Jesus], in the beginning laid the foundation of the earth, And the heavens are the work of Your hands. (Hebrews 1:10)

SCRIPTURE READINGS:

- Genesis 1
- Hebrews 11:1-3
- Hebrews 1:10-12

Questions? Learnings? Praises? Prayers? To Do's? Jesus is…?

DATE:

THE GARDEN — GOD'S PLAN FOR MARRIAGE

Jesus created humans to be unique: to bear God's image. Since God is a relationship (Father, Son, Spirit), He created humans for relationship (with God and people). You were created for relationships. The first relationship God created was marriage: one man and one woman for life. Jesus created marriage as a picture to the world of His love-filled relationship with the Church.

This [marriage] is a great mystery, but I speak concerning Christ and the church. (Ephesians 5:32)

SCRIPTURE READINGS:

- Genesis 2
- Matthew 19:3-6
- Ephesians 5:28-33

Questions? Learnings? Praises? Prayers? To Do's? Jesus is...?

3 READING

DATE:

4 READING

THE FALL — EVE'S DECEPTION, ADAM'S SIN, AND MANKIND'S CURSE

The Garden was life as God intended. God and people lived in perfect unity through God's love. But Satan lied. "You can have a life without God." Eve was deceived and sinned. Adam was not deceived. He knew and sinned. You are tempted to sin too. Sin divides, ruins, and kills things. Adam's disobedience brought death. Pause and thank God that Jesus' obedience offers life.

For if by the one man's [Adam's] offense death reigned through the one, much more those who receive abundance of grace and of the gift of righteousness will reign in life through the One, Jesus Christ. (Romans 5:17)

SCRIPTURE READINGS:

- Genesis 3
- 2 Corinthians 11:2-3
- Romans 5:12-21

Questions? Learnings? Praises? Prayers? To Do's? Jesus is...?

DATE:

CAIN AND ABEL — ABEL'S FAITH AND SACRIFICE VS. CAIN'S JEALOUSY AND HATRED

What did Adam and Eve talk about with their kids? They talked about God, the Garden, and their sin. Mom and dad shared how God accepted them because an innocent being was sacrificed (which foreshadowed the cross). Abel believed God about the innocent sacrifice. Cain tried to earn God's acceptance with his good works. Do you believe in Jesus' sacrifice for you?

> *By faith Abel offered to God a more excellent sacrifice than Cain, through which he obtained witness that he was righteous, God testifying of his gifts; and through it he being dead still speaks. (Hebrews 11:4)*

5 READING

SCRIPTURE READINGS:

- Genesis 4
- Hebrews 11:4
- 1 John 3:10-15

Questions? Learnings? Praises? Prayers? To Do's? Jesus is...?

DATE:

READING

ENOCH — ENOCH'S FAITH IN GOD AND MESSAGE TO THE WORLD

In a few generations, the world stopped following God. Enoch walked with God and called his generation to return to God. One day, as Enoch walked with God, he vanished. God took him to heaven. What does it mean to walk with Jesus? Jesus picks your direction for you. Your role is to love Him, keep your eyes on Him constantly, and stay close to Him wherever He leads you.

> *By faith Enoch was taken away so that he did not see death, "and was not found, because God had taken him"; for before he was taken he had this testimony, that he pleased God. (Hebrews 11:5)*

SCRIPTURE READINGS:

- Genesis 5:18-24
- Hebrews 11:5-6
- Jude 14-19

Questions? Learnings? Praises? Prayers? To Do's? Jesus is...?

DATE:

7
REFLECTION AND PRAYER

Look Back at Last Week — List what God did and what God taught you over the last week. This is your "thank God list" for next week.

Look Forward to Next Week — List what events, decisions, deadlines, or progress needs to happen in the next week. This is your prayer list for next week.

DATE:

8 READING

NOAH AND THE FLOOD — NOAH'S FAITH AND DELIVERANCE FROM THE FLOOD

When the world was corrupt and violent, God offered Noah grace (i.e. Jesus' undeserved love). God said it would rain when it never had. Noah believed God more than history, experts, or even himself. By faith, Noah and his family built a boat. Neighbors likely ridiculed them but God saved them. Like Noah, you are called to believe and obey God even when no one else does.

> *By faith Noah, being divinely warned of things not yet seen, moved with godly fear, prepared an ark for the saving of his household, by which he condemned the world and became heir of the righteousness which is according to faith. (Hebrews 11:7)*

SCRIPTURE READINGS:

- Genesis 6
- Genesis 7
- Hebrews 11:7

Questions? Learnings? Praises? Prayers? To Do's? Jesus is...?

DATE:

NOAH AND THE FLOOD — GOD'S JUDGMENT OF SIN AND JESUS' SECOND COMING

Noah was building a large boat when it had never rained. People likely thought, "Noah is crazy." But they went on with their lives. They planned their weddings, raised their kids, and built their careers. No one believed judgment was coming until it came. Jesus said His return to this world would be a complete surprise. You, like Noah, are called to believe God and not be surprised.

READING

But as the days of Noah were, so also will the coming of the Son of Man [Jesus] be. (Matthew 24:37)

SCRIPTURE READINGS:

- Genesis 8
- Genesis 9
- Matthew 24:36-44

Questions? Learnings? Praises? Prayers? To Do's? Jesus is...?

DATE:

10 READING

THE TOWER OF BABEL — LANGUAGE UNITES PEOPLE AGAINST GOD OR FOR GOD

The Tower of Babel was about society coming together to create unity without God. "Together we can fix this. Together we can." God protected the people from their sinful hearts by confusing their languages and scattering them. Today God uses the stars to declare His power and glory in every language. Today Jesus wants you to tell people that unity is only possible through Him.

> *"...we hear them speaking in our own tongues the wonderful works of God." So they were all amazed and perplexed, saying to one another, "Whatever could this mean?" (Acts 2:11–12)*

SCRIPTURE READINGS:

- Genesis 11:1-9
- Psalms 19:1-4
- Acts 2:1-21

Questions? Learnings? Praises? Prayers? To Do's? Jesus is...?

DATE:

JOB AND SATAN — JOB'S SUFFERING AND EXAMPLE OF PATIENCE

Job lost almost everything: his business, his life savings, his kids, and his health. Pause for a moment to imagine how you'd feel if you lost almost everything. Job agonized, cried out to God, and questioned God. But he never cursed God. In Job, you see how to cling to Jesus in faith and wait patiently on Him in your suffering. Believe the truth that God has compassion for you.

11 READING

My brethren, take the prophets, who spoke in the name of the Lord, as an example of suffering and patience. (James 5:10)

SCRIPTURE READINGS:

- Job 1
- Job 2
- James 5:9-11

Questions? Learnings? Praises? Prayers? To Do's? Jesus is…?

DATE:

12 READING

JOB AND ELIPHAZ — JOB'S SUFFERING AND FALSE ACCUSATIONS FROM HIS FRIENDS

Job's friends started well. For seven days, they sat with their friend in silence. Then Eliphaz, Bildad, and Zophar took turns accusing Job. Eventually Elihu accused him too. "What sin have you committed, Job? You can't be innocent." Job was innocent. Job reveals that it's okay for us to complain to God and question God when we are suffering. Jesus hears you and cares.

Why is light given to a man whose way is hidden, And whom God has hedged in? For my sighing comes before I eat, And my groanings pour out like water. (Job 3:23-24)

SCRIPTURE READINGS:

- Job 3
- Job 4
- Ezekiel 14:12-14

Questions? Learnings? Praises? Prayers? To Do's? Jesus is...?

DATE:

JOB AND ELIHU — JOB'S SUFFERING AND JOB'S FORESHADOWING OF CHRIST'S SUFFERING

Job suffered terribly but didn't realize that God was allowing him to be a prophetic picture of Jesus on the cross. Job cried out to God about things Jesus would experience: being innocent; falsely accused; struck on the cheek; delivered to the ungodly; weeping; bleeding; and dying. When you read Job, you're reading about what Jesus experienced on the cross for you.

13

READING

They gape at me with their mouth, They strike me reproachfully on the cheek, They gather together against me. God has delivered me to the ungodly, And turned me over to the hands of the wicked. (Job 16:10-11)

SCRIPTURE READINGS:

- Job 16
- Job 32
- Matthew 26:62-68

Questions? Learnings? Praises? Prayers? To Do's? Jesus is...?

DATE:

14
REFLECTION AND PRAYER

Look Back at Last Week — List what God did and what God taught you over the last week. This is your "thank God list" for next week.

Look Forward to Next Week — List what events, decisions, deadlines, or progress needs to happen in the next week. This is your prayer list for next week.

DATE:

JOB AND GOD — JOB'S SUFFERING AND GOD'S COMPASSIONATE MERCY

Job and his friends went back and forth. "You sinned." "How did I sin?" Then God spoke. Job responded to question after question with humility. "I don't know, God." "Only you can do that, God." Job's friends didn't respond like Job. In the end, God blessed Job once again. Job's story reminds you of God's compassion and mercy for His people. Jesus has compassion for you too.

15 READING

> *Indeed we count them blessed who endure. You have heard of the perseverance of Job and seen the end intended by the Lord—that the Lord [Jesus] is very compassionate and merciful. (James 5:11)*

SCRIPTURE READINGS:

- Job 38
- Job 42
- James 5:9-11

Questions? Learnings? Praises? Prayers? To Do's? Jesus is…?

DATE:

16 READING

ABRAHAM AND GOD'S CALL — ABRAHAM'S FAITH TO FOLLOW GOD AND THE PROMISE OF THE GOSPEL

If God called you to move but didn't tell you where you were moving, would you do it? God called Abraham that way. Abraham believed God so much he moved, eventually arriving in the Promised Land. God also revealed the gospel (or good news) to Abraham. In Abraham (in his descendant Jesus), all nations shall be blessed. You are blessed in God's promise to Abraham.

> *And the Scripture, foreseeing that God would justify the Gentiles by faith, preached the gospel to Abraham beforehand, saying, "In you [your descendant, Jesus] all the nations shall be blessed." (Galatians 3:8)*

SCRIPTURE READINGS:

- Genesis 12:1-9
- Hebrews 11:8-10
- Galatians 3:7-14

Questions? Learnings? Praises? Prayers? To Do's? Jesus is…?

DATE:

ABRAHAM AND DECEPTION — ABRAHAM'S FEAR OF PEOPLE VS. SARAH'S FAITH IN GOD

Abraham was terrified he would be killed for his wife, Sarah. Two times, Abraham asked Sarah not to reveal their marriage. Two times, leaders prepared to marry Sarah. Two times, Sarah waited on God to protect her. Two times, God supernaturally intervened. Sarah reveals the character of Jesus: a quiet and gentle spirit of submission with a steely-determination not to sin.

> *Do not let your adornment be merely outward— arranging the hair, wearing gold, or putting on fine apparel—4 rather let it be the hidden person [Jesus in you] of the heart, with the incorruptible beauty of a gentle and quiet spirit, which is very precious in the sight of God. (1 Peter 3:3–4)*

17 READING

SCRIPTURE READINGS:

- Genesis 12:10-20
- Genesis 20
- 1 Peter 3:1-6

Questions? Learnings? Praises? Prayers? To Do's? Jesus is…?

DATE:

18 READING

ABRAHAM AND LOT — LOT'S CHOICE OF LAND VS. ABRAHAM'S PROMISED LAND

Abraham and Lot made decisions differently. Lot chose his will: what made sense to him. Abraham chose God's will: what God said. How do you make decisions? God promised Abraham the land. Abraham lived believing God would fulfill His promises beyond his lifetime. You also are called to believe God's promises even when they're not in your timeframe.

> *And God gave him no inheritance in it, not even enough to set his foot on. But even when Abraham had no child, He promised to give it to him for a possession, and to his descendants after him. (Acts 7:5)*

SCRIPTURE READINGS:

- Genesis 13
- Nehemiah 9:6-8
- Acts 7:2-5

Questions? Learnings? Praises? Prayers? To Do's? Jesus is...?

DATE:

ABRAHAM AND MELCHISEDEK — ABRAHAM TITHES 10% TO MELCHISEDEK AND CHRIST'S PRIESTHOOD

Abraham mobilized 318 servants to pursue an army and deliver his nephew Lot from captivity. After the victory, Melchizedek met Abraham. Melchizedek pictured Jesus: the king and priest headquartered in Salem (or Jerusalem) who blesses people. Then Abraham tithed 10% of all he received. Before there was a law, people knew tithing (10%) was the starting point for giving.

19 READING

> (..."The Lord has sworn And will not relent, 'You [Jesus] are a priest forever According to the order of Melchizedek' "), by so much more Jesus has become a surety of a better covenant [the New Testament]. (Hebrews 7:21–22)

SCRIPTURE READINGS:

- Genesis 14
- Hebrews 5:5-11
- Hebrews 7:1-22

Questions? Learnings? Praises? Prayers? To Do's? Jesus is...?

DATE:

20 READING

ABRAHAM AND GOD'S PROMISE — ABRAHAM'S FAITH IN GOD AND GOD'S UNILATERAL COVENANT

God counted Abraham's faith in God's promise as righteousness. You are saved the same way. God counts your faith in Jesus' death and resurrection as righteousness. Have you believed? Then God made a covenant with Abraham and promised to fulfill His promises unilaterally. God sealed His covenant like those in Biblical times, by passing between the pieces of a sacrifice.

> *Now it was not written for his [Abraham's] sake alone that it was imputed to him, 24 but also for us. It shall be imputed to us who believe in Him who raised up Jesus our Lord from the dead, (Romans 4:23–24)*

SCRIPTURE READINGS:

- Genesis 15
- Jeremiah 34:18-20
- Romans 4

Questions? Learnings? Praises? Prayers? To Do's? Jesus is…?

DATE:

21
REFLECTION AND PRAYER

Look Back at Last Week — List what God did and what God taught you over the last week. This is your "thank God list" for next week.

Look Forward to Next Week — List what events, decisions, deadlines, or progress needs to happen in the next week. This is your prayer list for next week.

DATE:

22 READING

ABRAHAM AND HAGAR/ISHMAEL — ABRAHAM DOUBTS GOD'S PROMISE AND GOD BLESSES ISHMAEL

God promised Abraham and Sarah would have a child. After many years of trying, Sarah offered her maidservant, Hagar. Abraham agreed. Ishmael was born. Have you ever tried to fix something instead of waiting on God? God blessed Ishmael but conflict ensued for generations. Christ in you leads you to live by faith instead of controlling things in your power and strength.

> *For it is written that Abraham had two sons: the one by a bondwoman [Hagar], the other by a freewoman [Sarah]. But he who was of the bondwoman was born according to the flesh [human effort], and he of the freewoman through promise [faith in God], (Galatians 4:22–23)*

SCRIPTURE READINGS:

- Genesis 16
- Genesis 21:8-21
- Galatians 4:21-31

Questions? Learnings? Praises? Prayers? To Do's? Jesus is…?

DATE:

ABRAHAM AND CIRCUMCISION — THE SIGN OF CIRCUMCISION VS. SPIRITUAL CIRCUMCISION

When Abraham was 99, God gave him circumcision as a sign of the covenant. Circumcision is cutting away a part of the flesh. Physical circumcision in the Old Testament pictured spiritual circumcision (salvation) in the New Testament. When you receive Jesus as Savior, God cuts away your flesh from you. In Christ, you have been set free from your old, sinful nature.

23 READING

In Him [Jesus] you were also circumcised [spiritually] with the circumcision made without hands, by putting off the body of the sins of the flesh, by the circumcision of Christ, (Colossians 2:11)

SCRIPTURE READINGS:

- Genesis 17
- Romans 4:7-13
- Colossians 2:11-13

Questions? Learnings? Praises? Prayers? To Do's? Jesus is…?

DATE:

24 READING

ABRAHAM AND HIS THREE VISITORS — THE LORD VISITS ABRAHAM AND SODOM'S SINFULNESS

Jesus and two angels looked like three men when they visited Abraham. When Jesus sent the angels to Sodom and revealed His plan to judge the city, Abraham prayed. He asked Jesus to spare the city if there were ten righteous people (Lot had ten or more). Jesus agreed. Abraham pictured you spending time alone with Jesus and praying fervently for people who need Him.

...And they declare their sin as Sodom; They do not hide it. Woe to their soul! For they have brought evil upon themselves. (Isaiah 3:9)

SCRIPTURE READINGS:

- Genesis 18
- Isaiah 3:8-11
- Hebrews 13:1-2

Questions? Learnings? Praises? Prayers? To Do's? Jesus is...?

DATE:

LOT AND SODOM — THE LORD DELIVERS LOT AND JUDGES THE CITY OF SODOM

Jesus' angels looked like two men arriving in Sodom. The men of Sodom wanted to violate them. Lot offered his unmarried daughters instead. The angels took Lot, his wife, and his two unmarried daughters out of the city before it was judged. Jesus said the world would look like Sodom when He returns: living life, accepting sin, and not worrying about God's judgment.

25 READING

> *Likewise as it was also in the days of Lot: They ate, they drank, they bought, they sold, they planted, they built; but on the day that Lot went out of Sodom it rained fire and brimstone from heaven and destroyed them all. Even so will it be in the day when the Son of Man is revealed. (Luke 17:28–30)*

SCRIPTURE READINGS:

- Genesis 19
- Luke 17:28-36
- 2 Peter 2:6-9

Questions? Learnings? Praises? Prayers? To Do's? Jesus is…?

DATE:

READING 26

SARAH AND ISAAC — SARAH'S FAITH IN GOD AND ISAAC'S PROMISED BIRTH

When Sarah first heard that she would have a son in her old age, she laughed in unbelief. Then she started believing God. When she had her son, she laughed again for joy at all God did. She even named her son "laughter." Isaac means laughter. Sarah reminds you that, no matter how you have doubted God in the past, it's never too late for you to start believing Jesus' word.

> *By faith Sarah herself also received strength to conceive seed, and she bore a child when she was past the age, because she judged Him faithful who had promised. (Hebrews 11:11)*

SCRIPTURE READINGS:

- Genesis 21:1-7
- Romans 9:6-9
- Hebrews 11:11-16

Questions? Learnings? Praises? Prayers? To Do's? Jesus is...?

DATE:

ABRAHAM AND ISAAC — ABRAHAM'S SACRIFICE OF ISAAC FORESHADOWS CHRIST'S SACRIFICE ON THE CROSS

God promised Abraham he would have descendants through Isaac. Now God told Abraham to sacrifice his son. This pictured God the Father sacrificing Jesus for you. Isaac went willingly, carrying the wood (cross) to the place of sacrifice. Abraham believed that, even if Isaac died, God would resurrect him. Finally God provided a ram (picturing Christ) as a substitute sacrifice.

27
READING

By faith Abraham [like God the Father], when he was tested, offered up Isaac, and he who had received the promises offered up his only begotten son [like Jesus], (Hebrews 11:17)

SCRIPTURE READINGS:

- Genesis 22
- Romans 8:31-39
- Hebrews 11:17-19

Questions? Learnings? Praises? Prayers? To Do's? Jesus is...?

DATE:

28
REFLECTION AND PRAYER

Look Back at Last Week — List what God did and what God taught you over the last week. This is your "thank God list" for next week.

Look Forward to Next Week — List what events, decisions, deadlines, or progress needs to happen in the next week. This is your prayer list for next week.

DATE:

ISAAC AND REBEKAH — THE SERVANT'S PRAYER FOR GOD'S DIRECTION AND GOD'S GUIDANCE

God promised Isaac would have descendants. Isaac needed a bride. As Abraham's servant prayed for God's guidance in very specific ways, God answered. One way Jesus reveals Himself to you is by answering your very specific prayers for His wisdom and guidance. This story also pictured how the Holy Spirit (servant) draws the Church (bride) to Jesus (groom).

Trust in the Lord [Jesus] with all your heart, And lean not on your own understanding; In all your ways acknowledge Him, And He shall direct your paths. (Proverbs 3:5-6)

SCRIPTURE READINGS:

- Genesis 24
- Psalms 37:3-8
- Proverbs 3:5-6

Questions? Learnings? Praises? Prayers? To Do's? Jesus is…?

DATE:

30 READING

ESAU AND THE BIRTHRIGHT — GOD'S CHOOSES THE SECOND BIRTH AND ESAU'S SHORTSIGHTED TRADE

Being born before Isaac, Esau had the birthright (i.e. family leadership, twice the inheritance, etc.). One day, he was hungry. You often face the same challenge. Do you indulge a short-term urge or refrain for long-term benefit? Esau sold his birthright for a moment of pleasure. The good news is the grace of Christ is enough for you to be content in Him and not follow Esau.

looking carefully lest anyone fall short of the grace of God; lest any root of bitterness springing up cause trouble, and by this many become defiled; lest there be any fornicator or profane person like Esau, who for one morsel of food sold his birthright. (Hebrews 12:15–16)

SCRIPTURE READINGS:

- Genesis 25
- Romans 9:10-12
- Hebrews 12:14-17

Questions? Learnings? Praises? Prayers? To Do's? Jesus is…?

DATE:

ISAAC AND THE BLESSING — ISAAC INHERITS THE BLESSINGS GOD GAVE TO ABRAHAM

Isaac heard his dad talk about God's promise that his descendants would bless every nation on earth. One day, God told Isaac directly, "I am giving you the promises I made to your dad." God went further. "I am with you. You never have to be afraid." You, like Isaac, are a child of God's promises. Celebrate how Jesus has turned your parent's or discipler's faith into your faith today.

And the Lord [Jesus] appeared to him [Isaac] the same night and said, "I am the God of your father Abraham; do not fear, for I am with you. I will bless you and multiply your descendants for My servant Abraham's sake." (Genesis 26:24)

SCRIPTURE READINGS:

- Genesis 26
- 1 Chronicles 16:14-22
- Galatians 4:28

Questions? Learnings? Praises? Prayers? To Do's? Jesus is...?

DATE:

32 READING

JACOB AND THE BLESSING — JACOB DECEIVING OTHERS AND BEING DECEIVED BY OTHERS (SOWING AND REAPING)

Mom was teaching her child how to deceive. As Isaac was about to pass on his blessing, Jacob and Rebekah deceived Isaac. Isaac blessed Jacob instead of Esau. Later Jacob would be deceived by his father-in-law. Whatever you sow, you'll reap. If you sow to your old nature, you'll reap the consequences. If you invest in loving and following Jesus, you'll reap His life and joy.

Do not be deceived, God is not mocked; for whatever a man sows, that he will also reap. (Galatians 6:7)

SCRIPTURE READINGS:

- Genesis 27
- Genesis 29:21-25
- Galatians 6:7-8

Questions? Learnings? Praises? Prayers? To Do's? Jesus is...?

DATE:

JACOB AND THE LADDER — PEOPLE CONNECTING TO HEAVEN THROUGH A LADDER (I.E. THROUGH JESUS)

God is there with you right now. Are you aware? On a trip, Jacob dreamed about a ladder connecting earth to heaven. Then God told Jacob that the promises He gave to Abraham and Isaac were now his. Jacob awoke stunned by God's presence and promises. Jesus is our ladder. Your connection to heaven is Jesus. He is there with you right now. Are you aware?

33 READING

> *Then Jacob awoke from his sleep and said, "Surely the Lord [Jesus] is in this place, and I did not know it." (Genesis 28:16)*

SCRIPTURE READINGS:

- Genesis 28
- Psalms 105:4-12
- John 1:49-51

Questions? Learnings? Praises? Prayers? To Do's? Jesus is...?

DATE:

34 READING

JACOB AND LEAH/RACHEL — LEAH AND RACHEL STRUGGLE WITH EACH OTHER AND ARE USED BY GOD

God used Leah, Rachel, and their maids to give birth to the 12 sons who became the 12 tribes of Israel. The path was painful. Leah thought, "If we have kids, my husband will start loving me." Rachel said, "Give me a child or I'll die." God was with them in their pain. God cared deeply that Leah felt unloved. God heard Rachel's prayers. Jesus cares for you too. He hears you too.

When the Lord [Jesus] saw that Leah was unloved, He opened her womb; but Rachel was barren… Then God remembered Rachel, and God listened to her and opened her womb. (Genesis 29:31, 30:22)

SCRIPTURE READINGS:

- Genesis 29
- Genesis 30
- Ruth 4:10-11

Questions? Learnings? Praises? Prayers? To Do's? Jesus is…?

DATE:

35
REFLECTION AND PRAYER

Look Back at Last Week — List what God did and what God taught you over the last week. This is your "thank God list" for next week.

Look Forward to Next Week — List what events, decisions, deadlines, or progress needs to happen in the next week. This is your prayer list for next week.

DATE:

36 READING

JACOB AND THE WRESTLING — JACOB WRESTLING WITH GOD AND EMBRACING GOD AS HIS OWN

Jacob was moving home where he lied to steal Esau's blessing. Esau approached with an army. Jacob was terrified. Have you ever wrestled with fear? Control? God? That night, Jacob wrestled Jesus. Jesus asked, "What's your name?" This time, Jacob didn't lie. "Jacob." Jesus renamed him Israel. Jesus is close when you cling to Him in brokenness, humility, and honesty.

So He [Jesus] said to him, "What is your name?" He said, "Jacob [supplanter, schemer]." And He said, "Your name shall no longer be called Jacob, but Israel; for you have struggled with God and with men, and have prevailed." (Genesis 32:27–28)

SCRIPTURE READINGS:

- Genesis 32
- Genesis 33
- Hosea 12:2-6

Questions? Learnings? Praises? Prayers? To Do's? Jesus is...?

DATE:

JOSEPH AND HIS BETRAYAL — JOSEPH IS ENVIED, BETRAYED, AND SOLD BY HIS BROTHERS (LIKE JESUS WAS)

Many Old Testament characters foreshadowed Jesus. Theologians call them "types." Reading about Joseph is like reading about Jesus. Both were beloved sons of an ancient father. Both heard from God. Both were attacked by jealous children of Israel and falsely accused. Both had people plot their death and sell them for silver. Pause and thank God for Jesus' love for you.

37

READING

And the patriarchs, becoming envious, sold Joseph into Egypt. But God was with him [like God was with Jesus] (Acts 7:9)

SCRIPTURE READINGS:

- Genesis 37
- Acts 7:8-9
- Matthew 27:1-18

Questions? Learnings? Praises? Prayers? To Do's? Jesus is…?

DATE:

READING 38

JOSEPH AND POTIPHAR'S WIFE — JOSEPH AVOIDING AND FLEEING FROM SEXUAL TEMPTATION

Joseph was being tempted by his boss' wife. Day after day she pursued him. "No one will know." God would know. God created the intimacy between a husband and wife to picture Jesus and His church. How did Joseph respond? He avoided being alone with his temptation. He fled. May you love Jesus so much that you run from what's tempting your heart away from Him.

Flee sexual immorality... Or do you not know that your body is the temple of the Holy Spirit who is in you, whom you have from God, and you are not your own? (1 Corinthians 6:18–19)

SCRIPTURE READINGS:

- Genesis 39
- Proverbs 7
- 1 Corinthians 6:18-20

Questions? Learnings? Praises? Prayers? To Do's? Jesus is...?

DATE:

JOSEPH AND INTERPRETING DREAMS — JOSEPH'S TESTING IN PRISON AND PROMOTION BY PHARAOH

39

READING

Joseph pictured Jesus when he was betrayed and detained but innocent. Why does God allow you to suffer? To test and grow your faith. A baker and butler dreamed in jail, Joseph interpreted their dreams then waited two more years in jail. Pharaoh dreamed. Joseph interpreted his dream. Then Joseph began his life of public service at 30 like Jesus did around 30 years old.

> *He sent a man before them— Joseph—who was sold as a slave... Until the time that his word came to pass, The word of the Lord tested him. (Psalm 105:17, 19)*

SCRIPTURE READINGS:

- Genesis 40
- Genesis 41
- Psalms 105:13-22

Questions? Learnings? Praises? Prayers? To Do's? Jesus is...?

DATE:

TIM HOWEY | 45

40 READING

JOSEPH AND MEETING HIS BROTHERS — JOSEPH WEEPING FOR HIS BROTHERS (LIKE JESUS DID)

When you read about Joseph, you learn about Jesus and realize how much Jesus loves you. Joseph was second-in-charge to Pharaoh (like Jesus with God the Father). Joseph's brothers bowed their knees to him (like all will bow to Jesus). Joseph wept with love over his brothers' blindness (like Jesus wept for Jerusalem). Pause and thank Jesus for His great love for you.

Now as He [Jesus] drew near, He saw the city and wept over it, saying, "If you had known, even you, especially in this your day, the things that make for your peace! But now they are hidden from your eyes. (Luke 19:41–42)

SCRIPTURE READINGS:

- Genesis 42
- Genesis 43
- Luke 19:41-42

Questions? Learnings? Praises? Prayers? To Do's? Jesus is...?

DATE:

JOSEPH AND HIS REVELATION — JOSEPH REVEALS HIS IDENTITY (LIKE JESUS WILL) AT THE SECOND COMING

When you read about Joseph, you learn about Jesus and grow in awe of Him. Joseph revealed himself at his brothers' second visit (like Jesus will reveal Himself at His second coming). God allowed Joseph's betrayal to save the world (like God did with Jesus). Joseph gathered his family under his leadership and provision (like Jesus). Pause and reflect on how great Jesus is.

41 READING

> *But now, do not therefore be grieved or angry with yourselves because you sold me [Joseph] here; for God sent me [like Jesus] before you to preserve life. (Genesis 45:5)*

SCRIPTURE READINGS:

- Genesis 44
- Genesis 45
- Acts 7:9-13

Questions? Learnings? Praises? Prayers? To Do's? Jesus is...?

DATE:

42
REFLECTION AND PRAYER

Look Back at Last Week — List what God did and what God taught you over the last week. This is your "thank God list" for next week.

Look Forward to Next Week — List what events, decisions, deadlines, or progress needs to happen in the next week. This is your prayer list for next week.

DATE:

JOSEPH AND CARING FOR FAMILY — GOD USES JOSEPH'S SUFFERING (LIKE JESUS' SUFFERING) FOR OTHERS

All things work together for good to those who love God. God used many bad things that happened to Joseph — betrayal, enslavement, false accusation, imprisonment — to work for good. Joseph was able to save his family. That was good. What problems are you facing? Love God. Jesus promises He will use all things together for good if you love God. Do you love God?

And we know that all things work together for good to those who love God, to those who are the called according to His purpose. (Romans 8:28)

SCRIPTURE READINGS:

- Genesis 46
- Genesis 47
- Romans 8:28

Questions? Learnings? Praises? Prayers? To Do's? Jesus is…?

DATE:

44 READING

JACOB AND THE BLESSINGS — JACOB PASSES ON GOD'S BLESSING BEFORE HE DIES

Jacob was near death but strong in faith. Jacob believed God would be faithful to him even after death and bring Israel back to the Promised Land. By faith, Jacob blessed his grandsons. By faith, Jacob charged them about bringing back his bones. Jacob faced his death in faith. God designed you to never stop growing in faith where the last days of life are your most faith-filled.

> *By faith Jacob, when he was dying, blessed each of the sons of Joseph, and worshiped, leaning on the top of his staff. (Hebrews 11:21)*

SCRIPTURE READINGS:

- Genesis 48
- Genesis 49:29-33
- Hebrews 11:20-21

Questions? Learnings? Praises? Prayers? To Do's? Jesus is...?

DATE:

JOSEPH AND HIS DEATH — THE FEAR OF JOSEPH'S BROTHERS VS. THE FORGIVENESS OF JOSEPH

The brothers wondered, "Now that dad's gone, will Joseph take revenge?" Joseph forgave them. Why do we forgive? Not because people apologize the right way, or feel bad enough, or deserve forgiveness. Christians forgive because we have been forgiven. Forgiveness is you, like God, accepting the suffering of Jesus as payment. Who does God want you to forgive?

Let all bitterness, wrath, anger, clamor, and evil speaking be put away from you, with all malice. And be kind to one another, tenderhearted, forgiving one another, even as God in Christ forgave you. (Ephesians 4:31–32)

SCRIPTURE READINGS:

- Genesis 50
- Ephesians 4:31-32
- Hebrews 11:22

Questions? Learnings? Praises? Prayers? To Do's? Jesus is...?

DATE:

46 READING

THE MIDWIVES' DILEMMA — WHEN SHOULD PEOPLE DISOBEY THE GOVERNMENT?

When does God want you to disobey the government? When they try to force you personally to disobey God. Israel was enslaved but growing. Pharaoh commanded the midwives to kill the newborn boys. The midwives disobeyed the government. The way you follow Jesus is to obey every law (even laws you disagree with) until they try to force you personally to disobey God.

But Peter and the other apostles answered and said: "We ought to obey God rather than men. (Acts 5:29)

SCRIPTURE READINGS:

- Exodus 1
- Acts 4:18-20
- Acts 5:26-32

Questions? Learnings? Praises? Prayers? To Do's? Jesus is…?

DATE:

MOSES AND HIS CHILDHOOD — THE FAITH OF MOSES' PARENTS AND MOSES FLEES EGYPT

Do you live by faith in Christ? Moses' parents believed God so much they were unafraid of the government. Moses believed God so much he chose deprivation with God's people instead of luxury with the Egyptians. Are you willing to wait on Jesus? Moses stopped waiting on God and tried to deliver Israel in his own strength. Loving Jesus is both believing and waiting on Him.

47

READING

By faith Moses, when he was born, was hidden three months by his parents, because they saw he was a beautiful child; and they were not afraid of the king's command. (Hebrews 11:23)

SCRIPTURE READINGS:

- Exodus 2
- Acts 7:17-29
- Hebrews 11:23-26

Questions? Learnings? Praises? Prayers? To Do's? Jesus is...?

DATE:

48 READING

MOSES AND THE BURNING BUSH — GOD CALLS MOSES AND MOSES GIVES VARIOUS EXCUSES

After 40 years as a shepherd, Moses saw a burning bush. God said, "You will deliver My people from Egypt." Moses gave excuses. "Who am I? Who do I say sent me? What if they won't listen? I'm not a good speaker." God patiently addressed each concern. When Moses said, "Get someone else," God got angry. What's Jesus been prompting you to do? Love Him and follow.

> Now therefore, go, and I will be with your mouth and teach you what you shall say." 13 But he said, "O my Lord, please send by the hand of whomever else You may send." 14 So the anger of the Lord was kindled against Moses... (Exodus 4:12-14)

SCRIPTURE READINGS:

- Exodus 3
- Exodus 4
- Acts 7:30-36

Questions? Learnings? Praises? Prayers? To Do's? Jesus is...?

DATE:

49
REFLECTION AND PRAYER

Look Back at Last Week — List what God did and what God taught you over the last week. This is your "thank God list" for next week.

Look Forward to Next Week — List what events, decisions, deadlines, or progress needs to happen in the next week. This is your prayer list for next week.

DATE:

50 READING

MOSES AND PHARAOH — GOD'S MESSAGE TO PHARAOH AND PHARAOH'S ARROGANT REJECTION

Moses told Pharaoh that God said, "Let My people go." Instead of letting them go, Pharaoh made life worse. Israel asked Moses, "How could you?" Moses asked God, "How could You?" Then God told Moses that knowing Him was more important than being comfortable. God said, "Know that I am the LORD your God." Do you know Jesus is Almighty God? Is He your God?

> *I will take you as My people, and I will be your God. Then you shall know that I am the Lord your God who brings you out from under the burdens of the Egyptians. (Exodus 6:7)*

SCRIPTURE READINGS:

- Exodus 5
- Exodus 6:1-13
- Nehemiah 9:9-10

Questions? Learnings? Praises? Prayers? To Do's? Jesus is...?

DATE:

MOSES AND THE MIRACLES — GOD REVEALS HIMSELF THROUGH MIRACLES AND PLAGUES

Why would Pharaoh let God's people go? He didn't believe in God and profited from their slave labor. God used ten mighty plagues to reveal His sovereign power over nature and Egypt's false gods: blood, frogs, lice, flies, etc. God accomplished His larger goal too. "The Egyptians shall know that I am the LORD." The whole world will know that no one can stop the Almighty God.

51 READING

And the Egyptians shall know that I am the Lord, when I stretch out My hand on Egypt and bring out the children of Israel from among them." (Exodus 7:5)

SCRIPTURE READINGS:

- Exodus 7
- Exodus 8
- Psalms 105:23-38

Questions? Learnings? Praises? Prayers? To Do's? Jesus is...?

DATE:

52 READING

MOSES AND THE PASSOVER — THE ORIGIN OF THE PASSOVER LAMB AND JESUS OUR PASSOVER LAMB

Reading about Passover is like reading about Jesus. Each house found a spotless male lamb (like Jesus was our sinless Lamb). They killed the lamb and put his blood on the door (like Jesus was crucified on the cross). When God saw the blood, judgment would "pass over" them (picturing total forgiveness through Christ). Jesus went to the cross for you as your Lamb.

Therefore purge out the old leaven [yeast], that you may be a new lump, since you truly are unleavened. For indeed Christ, our Passover, was sacrificed for us. (1 Corinthians 5:7)

SCRIPTURE READINGS:

- Exodus 11
- Exodus 12
- 1 Corinthians 5:7

Questions? Learnings? Praises? Prayers? To Do's? Jesus is...?

DATE:

MOSES AND THE RED SEA — MOSES' FAITH AT THE PASSOVER AND CROSSING THE RED SEA

Have you ever faced a situation that looked hopeless? That's the Red Sea. God delivered Israel from slavery but Pharaoh decided to enslave them again. Armies bore down on one side and the Red Sea blocked the other. There was no way out unless God moved. Jesus allows you to face situations beyond your control to help you realize you were never in control. Jesus is.

53

READING

By faith he [Moses] kept the Passover and the sprinkling of blood, lest he who destroyed the firstborn should touch them. By faith they passed through the Red Sea as by dry land, whereas the Egyptians, attempting to do so, were drowned. (Hebrews 11:28–29)

SCRIPTURE READINGS:

- Exodus 13
- Exodus 14
- Hebrews 11:24-29

Questions? Learnings? Praises? Prayers? To Do's? Jesus is…?

DATE:

READING 54

MOSES AND HIS SONGS — THREE OF MOSES' SONGS IN SCRIPTURE

Jesus created you to sing about how great He is and all He has done. Do you sing to Him? He listens to you with joy. Songs help you love Jesus with all your heart, mind, soul, and strength. When God saved Israel at the Red Sea, Moses wrote a song. The people sang it with relief, joy and thankfulness. Then Moses wrote a second song and a third. Why not sing to God now?

> *Then Moses and the children of Israel sang this song to the Lord, and spoke, saying: "I will sing to the Lord, For He has triumphed gloriously! The horse and its rider He has thrown into the sea! (Exodus 15:1)*

SCRIPTURE READINGS:

- Exodus 15
- Psalms 90
- Revelation 15:1-4

Questions? Learnings? Praises? Prayers? To Do's? Jesus is...?

DATE:

MOSES AND THE MANNA — THE BREAD FROM HEAVEN AND THE WORD OF GOD

Israel ran out of food. Each morning a flour-like dust covered the ground. "What?" They called it "what" (in Hebrew "manna"). It was their food. Each tent gathered food for the day before the sun burned it away. God was testing and feeding them. Would they choose to follow God and eat that day or not? The Bible is your manna: your spiritual food, your spiritual test, each day.

55 READING

But He [Jesus] answered and said, "It is written, 'Man shall not live by bread alone, but by every word that proceeds from the mouth of God.' " (Matthew 4:4)

SCRIPTURE READINGS:

- Exodus 16
- Deuteronomy 8
- Matthew 4:1-4

Questions? Learnings? Praises? Prayers? To Do's? Jesus is…?

DATE:

56
REFLECTION AND PRAYER

Look Back at Last Week — List what God did and what God taught you over the last week. This is your "thank God list" for next week.

Look Forward to Next Week — List what events, decisions, deadlines, or progress needs to happen in the next week. This is your prayer list for next week.

DATE:

MOSES AND WATER THE ROCK — MOSES STRIKES THE ROCK (I.E. CHRIST) FOR LIFE-GIVING WATER

Israel ran out of water. They faced death. Israel cried out, "Moses, are you trying to kill us?" Moses prayed, "What do I do?" God said, "Strike the rock with your rod. Water will come out." When you read about the rock, you're reading about Jesus. We too were facing death. Jesus is the Rock that God struck at the cross so life came out. Jesus is the Rock struck to save you.

57

READING

> *all were baptized into Moses in the cloud and in the sea, all ate the same spiritual food, and all drank the same spiritual drink. For they drank of that spiritual Rock that followed them, and that Rock was Christ. (1 Corinthians 10:2–4)*

SCRIPTURE READINGS:

- Exodus 17:1-7
- Psalms 78:12-25
- 1 Corinthians 10:1-4

Questions? Learnings? Praises? Prayers? To Do's? Jesus is…?

DATE:

58 READING

MOSES AND HOLDING UP HIS ARMS — ISRAEL'S WARFARE AND MOSES' PRAYER (SUPPORTED BY OTHERS)

As long as Moses held his hands up to God, God gave Israel victory. Whenever Moses let his hands down, Israel was defeated. That's what prayer is for you. Prayer is looking to Jesus instead of people. Prayer is admitting you can't but Jesus can. Prayer is asking God to move. Moses needed friends to lift up his hands. God designed us to support each other in prayer.

And so it was, when Moses held up his hand, that Israel prevailed; and when he let down his hand, Amalek prevailed. (Exodus 17:11)

SCRIPTURE READINGS:

- Exodus 17:8-15
- Deuteronomy 25:17-19
- 1 Timothy 2:8

Questions? Learnings? Praises? Prayers? To Do's? Jesus is...?

DATE:

MOSES AND DELEGATION — MOSES IS OVERWHELMED AND THE IMPORTANCE OF OTHERS

What happens when you try to do more than God wants? Progress slows. People get frustrated. You wear down. Moses was working from early in the morning to late at night. Jethro said, "Share the load. Let others help. You can't do this alone." Christians are parts of Christ's body. When you do your God-given role and others do theirs, the body works and Jesus is glorified.

59

READING

So Moses' father-in-law said to him, "The thing that you do is not good. Both you and these people who are with you will surely wear yourselves out. For this thing is too much for you; you are not able to perform it by yourself." (Exodus 18:17–18)

SCRIPTURE READINGS:

- Exodus 18
- Numbers 11:14-30
- Ecclesiastes 4:9-12

Questions? Learnings? Praises? Prayers? To Do's? Jesus is…?

DATE:

60 READING

ISRAEL AND A SPECIAL PEOPLE — ISRAEL (AND THE CHURCH) IS A SPECIAL PEOPLE AND KINGDOM OF PRIESTS

God called Israel to be His special people. God wanted to make them uniquely like Him. When the nations saw Israel, God wanted them to see Him, His holiness, His differentness. Israel was to be a kingdom of priests, connecting the nations with God. God made Christians His special people too. When people see you, do they see Jesus? Are people being drawn to Jesus?

> *But you are a chosen generation, a royal priesthood, a holy nation, His own special people, that you may proclaim the praises of Him [Jesus] who called you out of darkness into His marvelous light; (1 Peter 2:9)*

SCRIPTURE READINGS:

- Exodus 19
- Deuteronomy 7:6-11
- 1 Peter 2:4-12

Questions? Learnings? Praises? Prayers? To Do's? Jesus is...?

DATE:

THE 10 COMMANDMENTS — LOVE FULFILLS THE LAW AND THE IMPLICATION OF BREAKING ONE LAW

On Mount Sinai, God gave Moses the 10 commandments. All 10 were about love. Four were about loving God. For example, you can't love God if you have gods before Him. Six were about loving people. For example, you can't love people if you're stealing from them. God wants you to love Him with all your heart, soul, and mind and love your neighbor as yourself. That's Jesus.

For the commandments, "You shall not commit adultery," "You shall not murder," "You shall not steal," "You shall not bear false witness," "You shall not covet," and if there is any other commandment, are all summed up in this saying, namely, "You shall love your neighbor as yourself." (Romans 13:9)

SCRIPTURE READINGS:

- Exodus 20
- Romans 13:8-10
- James 2:8-11

Questions? Learnings? Praises? Prayers? To Do's? Jesus is…?

DATE:

62 READING

THE OLD TESTAMENT LAWS — THE LAW LEADS PEOPLE TO CHRIST AND THE TWO MOST IMPORTANT LAWS

God gave Moses the 10 commandments and many more (613 total). What did the Law of Moses do? The Law revealed God's beauty, perfection, holiness, and love. The Law also exposed our human sinfulness, weakness, and failure. The Law revealed that we cannot be good on our own. We needed Jesus to keep the Law for us and die for us. You need Jesus.

> *Therefore the law was our tutor to bring us to Christ, that we might be justified by faith. (Galatians 3:24)*

SCRIPTURE READINGS:

- Exodus 21
- Matthew 22:34-40
- Galatians 3:19-26

Questions? Learnings? Praises? Prayers? To Do's? Jesus is...?

DATE:

63

REFLECTION AND PRAYER

Look Back at Last Week — List what God did and what God taught you over the last week. This is your "thank God list" for next week.

Look Forward to Next Week — List what events, decisions, deadlines, or progress needs to happen in the next week. This is your prayer list for next week.

DATE:

64 READING

MOSES AND THE GOLDEN CALF — MOSES' ABSENCE FOR 40 DAYS AND ISRAEL'S IDOLATRY

Israel watched Moses hike up Mt. Sinai and disappear into the cloud. Days passed. Israel wondered, "Will he ever return?" In fear, they sought comfort in a "god" of this world. You were created to find all your joy and contentment in Christ. How quickly do we forget the God we can't see? Turn away from any "god" you're seeking comfort in. Find the comfort that's only in Jesus.

> They made a calf in Horeb, And worshiped the molded image. Thus they changed their glory Into the image of an ox that eats grass. They forgot God their Savior, Who had done great things in Egypt, (Psalm 106:19–21)

SCRIPTURE READINGS:

- Exodus 32
- Psalms 106:19-23
- Acts 7:37-43

Questions? Learnings? Praises? Prayers? To Do's? Jesus is...?

DATE:

MOSES AND SEEING GOD — MOSES' FACE SHINES WITH GOD'S GLORY AFTER BEING IN GOD'S PRESENCE

When you spend time with God, you're transformed and people notice. Moses spent weeks in God's presence on Mount Sinai. His face radiated the glory of God. He shined so much that he had to cover his face to avoid scaring people. When you spend time in God's presence, God changes you. People see God's glory shining through you. Do people see Jesus through you?

READING 65

> unlike Moses, who put a veil over his face so that the children of Israel could not look steadily at the end of what was passing away... But we all, with unveiled face, beholding as in a mirror the glory of the Lord, are being transformed into the same image from glory to glory, just as by the Spirit of the Lord. (2 Corinthians 3:13, 18)

SCRIPTURE READINGS:

- Exodus 33
- Exodus 34
- 2 Corinthians 3

Questions? Learnings? Praises? Prayers? To Do's? Jesus is...?

DATE:

66 READING

MOSES FINISHES THE TABERNACLE — THE EARTHLY TABERNACLE PICTURES GOD'S HEAVENLY TABERNACLE

God gave Moses a vision of heaven then said to build a portable worship center like what he saw. He called it the tabernacle. Every piece of furniture pictured your worship today. Every detail pictured Jesus. One entrance (Christ). Altar (cross). Wash basin/laver (confession). Lamp (Spirit). Bread (Bible). Incense (prayer). Ark (Christ). Priests with access to God (Christians).

> *Now this is the main point of the things we are saying: We have such a High Priest, who is seated at the right hand of the throne of the Majesty in the heavens... Moses was divinely instructed when he was about to make the tabernacle. For He said, "See that you make all things according to the pattern shown you on the mountain." (Hebrews 8:1, 5)*

SCRIPTURE READINGS:

- Exodus 40
- Hebrews 8:1-10
- Hebrews 9:1-15

Questions? Learnings? Praises? Prayers? To Do's? Jesus is…?

DATE:

THE SIN OFFERING — THE SIN OFFERING IN THE OLD TESTAMENT FORESHADOWS CHRIST'S SACRIFICE

In Leviticus, God revealed five offerings. All five pictured Jesus. Three were for worship: burnt, grain, and peace. Two were for forgiveness: sin and trespass. Only Christ makes it possible for you to worship God: showing Him what He's worth. Only Christ makes it possible for you to be forgiven: He paid for your sins. Jesus' sacrifice fulfilled and ended these sacrifices for you.

And every priest stands ministering daily and offering repeatedly the same sacrifices, which can never take away sins. But this Man, after He had offered one sacrifice for sins forever, sat down at the right hand of God, (Hebrews 10:11–12)

SCRIPTURE READINGS:

- Leviticus 4:1-12
- Hebrews 9:16-28
- Hebrews 10:1-18

Questions? Learnings? Praises? Prayers? To Do's? Jesus is...?

DATE:

68 READING

PRIESTS VS. NADAB/ABIHU — THE TRUE PRIESTS IN THE OLD (LEVITES) AND NEW (CHRISTIANS) TESTAMENTS

God is holy; separate; with stunning power, beauty, and perfection. God called Aaron's sons to be priests. Priests helped people worship in ways that respected God's holiness. Nadab and Abihu wanted to worship in their own way and died. Pause and thank Jesus for fulfilling the Old Testament. Now every Christian is a priest. God calls you to help people worship through Christ.

and [Jesus] has made us kings and priests to His God and Father, to Him be glory and dominion forever and ever. Amen. (Revelation 1:6)

SCRIPTURE READINGS:

- Leviticus 9
- Leviticus 10:1-7
- Revelation 1:5-6

Questions? Learnings? Praises? Prayers? To Do's? Jesus is...?

DATE:

LOVE YOUR NEIGHBOR — LOVE YOUR ENEMY, WHO IS YOUR NEIGHBOR, AND THE GOOD SAMARITAN

Jesus said the first commandments are to love God and love your neighbor. It's impossible to love your neighbor without loving God. Who is your neighbor? Anyone near you. Also those who irritate, dislike, or hurt you. Why love them? That's Jesus. In the Good Samaritan story, you were the one left for dead. Jesus was the Samaritan who loved His neighbor (you) as Himself.

69
READING

> *So he [a lawyer] answered and said, " 'You shall love the Lord your God with all your heart, with all your soul, with all your strength, and with all your mind,' and 'your neighbor as yourself.' " 28 And He [Jesus] said to him, "You have answered rightly; do this and you will live." (Luke 10:27–28)*

SCRIPTURE READINGS:

- Leviticus 19:18
- Matthew 5:43-48
- Luke 10:25-37

Questions? Learnings? Praises? Prayers? To Do's? Jesus is…?

DATE:

70
REFLECTION AND PRAYER

Look Back at Last Week — List what God did and what God taught you over the last week. This is your "thank God list" for next week.

Look Forward to Next Week — List what events, decisions, deadlines, or progress needs to happen in the next week. This is your prayer list for next week.

DATE:

THE PILLAR OF CLOUD AND FIRE — RELYING ON HUMAN GUIDANCE VS. GOD'S GUIDANCE

As Israel camped in the wilderness for 40 years, a giant smoke-and-fire pillar hovered in the sky. Israel didn't know what God wanted yet so they watched the pillar. If it stayed, they stayed. If it moved, they packed up camp. That's how we follow Jesus. We don't know what God wants yet so we watch Jesus. If He stays, we stay. If He moves, we follow. Are your eyes on the pillar?

> *At the command of the Lord [Jesus] the children of Israel would journey, and at the command of the Lord they would camp; as long as the cloud stayed above the tabernacle they remained encamped. (Numbers 9:18)*

SCRIPTURE READINGS:

- Numbers 9:15-23
- Numbers 10:29-36
- Isaiah 48:17-19

Questions? Learnings? Praises? Prayers? To Do's? Jesus is...?

DATE:

72 READING

THE PEOPLE'S COMPLAINING — ISRAEL'S COMPLAINING AND GOD'S JUDGMENT

Israel complained a lot about their food, leaders, life, etc. They complained instead of being thankful God freed them, led them, and fed them every day. Are you thanking God for what you have? Or are you complaining about what you don't have? Jesus wasn't a complainer. Jesus in you isn't a complainer. When you complain, you don't shine Jesus' light. You don't please God.

Do all things without complaining and disputing, that you may become blameless and harmless, children of God without fault in the midst of a crooked and perverse generation, among whom you shine as lights in the world, (Philippians 2:14–15)

SCRIPTURE READINGS:

- Numbers 11
- Numbers 12
- Philippians 2:14-16

Questions? Learnings? Praises? Prayers? To Do's? Jesus is...?

DATE:

THE 12 SPIES AND 40 DAYS OF SEARCHING — THE FEARS OF THE 10 SPIES VS. THE FAITH OF CALEB/JOSHUA

73 READING

Faith isn't tested when you're able. Faith is tested when you can't but God can. When God promised, "I am giving you the land," victory was certain. God sent 12 spies to see how big the victory would be, not see if they could win. Two spies believed God while ten said, "We are not able." Are you believing God? Your faith will grow when you believe God instead of your fears.

> *"Send men to spy out the land of Canaan, which I am giving to the children of Israel; from each tribe of their fathers you shall send a man, every one a leader among them." (Numbers 13:2)*

SCRIPTURE READINGS:

- Numbers 13
- Deuteronomy 1:19-28
- Joshua 14:6-9

Questions? Learnings? Praises? Prayers? To Do's? Jesus is...?

DATE:

74 READING

THE 12 SPIES AND 40 YEARS OF WANDERING — ISRAEL'S UNBELIEF AND GOD JUDGMENT

God promised to bring His people into the land to give them rest and show the world His power. When God's people didn't believe, an 11-day journey turned into 40 years of wandering. What happens when you live in fear? You miss out on seeing God move, experiencing Jesus' rest, and glorifying God. May you, like Joshua and Caleb, believe God's promises and act in faith.

Do not harden your hearts as in the rebellion, In the day of trial in the wilderness... So we see that they [Israel] could not enter in because of unbelief. (Hebrews 3:8, 19)

SCRIPTURE READINGS:

- Numbers 14
- Deuteronomy 1:29-46
- Hebrews 3

Questions? Learnings? Praises? Prayers? To Do's? Jesus is...?

DATE:

KORAH, DATHAN, AND ABIRAM — COMPLAINING ABOUT MOSES AND GOD'S JUDGMENT

Korah, Dathan, and Abiram were jealous of Moses. "Who put Moses in charge?" God did. When you rebel against the people God put in charge, you're not rebelling against them. You're actually rebelling against God. If Jesus lives in you, He leads you in a spirit of submission not rebellion. Do you sense submission or rebellion against the leaders God put in your life?

75 READING

> *But these speak evil of whatever they do not know; and whatever they know naturally, like brute beasts, in these things they corrupt themselves. Woe to them! For they have gone in the way of Cain, have run greedily in the error of Balaam for profit, and perished in the rebellion of Korah. (Jude 10–11)*

SCRIPTURE READINGS:

- Numbers 16
- Psalms 106:9-18
- Jude 10-11

Questions? Learnings? Praises? Prayers? To Do's? Jesus is…?

DATE:

READING 76

AARON'S ROD — GOD CHOOSES THE TRIBE OF LEVI AND FRUITFULNESS PROVES GOD'S CHOICE

God chose the tribe of Levi to manage the tabernacle, offer sacrifices, and lead worship. The other tribes of Israel complained. God proposed a test. God told each tribe to bring a wooden rod. The rod of dead wood that bore fruit would show God's choice. Aaron's rod pictured you. You, like the rod, were dead (spiritually). Is Jesus working inside you to bear fruit for Him?

For a good tree does not bear bad fruit, nor does a bad tree bear good fruit. For every tree is known by its own fruit. For men do not gather figs from thorns, nor do they gather grapes from a bramble bush. (Luke 6:43–44)

SCRIPTURE READINGS:

- Numbers 17
- Numbers 1:47-54
- Luke 6:43-45

Questions? Learnings? Praises? Prayers? To Do's? Jesus is...?

DATE:

77
REFLECTION AND PRAYER

Look Back at Last Week — List what God did and what God taught you over the last week. This is your "thank God list" for next week.

Look Forward to Next Week — List what events, decisions, deadlines, or progress needs to happen in the next week. This is your prayer list for next week.

DATE:

78 READING

THE PRIESTS AND TITHING — THE PEOPLE TITHE 10% AND THE PRIESTS TITHE 10%

Tithing is giving God the first 10% of all you receive. Tithing shows you believe God owns 100%. Long before the Law, people like Abraham and Jacob tithed (Genesis 14, 28). Then God gave Moses laws. Israel tithed 10% of everything they received. Priests tithed 10% of all the tithes they received. Does your giving show that you love Jesus and believe He owns everything?

Will a man rob God? Yet you have robbed Me! But you say, 'In what way have we robbed You?' In tithes and offerings. (Malachi 3:8)

SCRIPTURE READINGS:

- Numbers 18
- Deuteronomy 14:22-29
- Malachi 3:8-12

Questions? Learnings? Praises? Prayers? To Do's? Jesus is...?

DATE:

STRIKING THE ROCK TWICE — MOSES' ANGER WITH ISRAEL AND CHRIST THE ROCK (STRUCK ONCE AT THE CROSS)

Israel faced another water crisis. In Exodus 17, God said to strike the rock. This pictured Jesus stricken once for our sins at the cross. Now God said speak to the rock. This pictured praying to Jesus for help. In his anger, Moses struck the rock, dishonored Jesus, and lost the Promised Land. Your human anger never makes things better. Your human wrath does not honor Jesus.

79 READING

for the wrath of man does not produce the righteousness of God. (James 1:20)

SCRIPTURE READINGS:

- Numbers 20
- 1 Corinthians 10:1-4
- James 1:19-20

Questions? Learnings? Praises? Prayers? To Do's? Jesus is...?

DATE:

80 READING

THE BRONZE SERPENT — ISRAEL'S COMPLAINTS, GOD'S JUDGMENT, AND CHRIST ON THE CROSS

Israel was complaining about the food God miraculously provided every day. Fiery serpents slithered into camp and bit the people. Moses hung a bronze serpent on a pole so whoever looked would live. Jesus said this story pictured Him. The snake bites pictured our sin and death. The bronze serpent pictured Jesus on the cross. Have you looked to Jesus and lived?

And as Moses lifted up the serpent in the wilderness, even so must the Son of Man [Jesus] be lifted up, (John 3:14)

SCRIPTURE READINGS:

- Numbers 21:1-9
- John 3:14-17
- 1 Corinthians 10:5-12

Questions? Learnings? Praises? Prayers? To Do's? Jesus is…?

DATE:

BALAAM AND THE DONKEY — KING BALAK'S OFFER TO THE PROPHET BALAAM AND BALAAM'S GREED

King Balak was terrified of Israel so he tried to hire the prophet Balaam to curse them. First God told Balaam no. Then God told Balaam not to go unless they came again. Balaam was greedy and went anyway. God told him through a donkey, "Only say what I say." In Jesus, you can be content. You don't have to be like Balaam. Are you living completely content in Christ?

81 READING

> *They have forsaken the right way and gone astray, following the way of Balaam the son of Beor, who loved the wages of unrighteousness; but he was rebuked for his iniquity: a dumb donkey speaking with a man's voice restrained the madness of the prophet. (2 Peter 2:15–16)*

SCRIPTURE READINGS:

- Numbers 22
- Numbers 23
- 2 Peter 2:15-16

Questions? Learnings? Praises? Prayers? To Do's? Jesus is...?

DATE:

82 READING

PHINEHAS AND BAAL-PEOR — ISRAEL'S SIN AGAINST GOD AND PHINEHAS' PASSION FOR GOD

Balaam couldn't curse Israel so he taught Balak how to destroy them from the inside. "Offer them other gods and sex." Israel's sins brought a plague. People started dying. Phinehas was passionate about God and keeping Israel alive so he acted to stop it. Is something drawing your heart away from God? Let Jesus be your Phinehas, removing other loves from your heart.

> *But I have a few things against you, because you have there those who hold the doctrine of Balaam, who taught Balak to put a stumbling block before the children of Israel, to eat things sacrificed to idols, and to commit sexual immorality. (Revelation 2:14)*

SCRIPTURE READINGS:

- Numbers 25
- Psalms 106:24-31
- Revelation 2:14

Questions? Learnings? Praises? Prayers? To Do's? Jesus is...?

DATE:

THE STORY OF THEIR WANDERING — REVIEWING ISRAEL'S HISTORY AND THE WORD OF GOD

After 40 years, Moses was leading a new generation who needed to hear their story. God had promised to give the land to the parents but they doubted God. Now God promised to give the land to the children and bless them to draw all nations to Him. Jesus wants to do the same through you. He wants you to believe and obey Him and, through you, draw people to Him.

83
READING

> *"For the Lord your God has blessed you in all the work of your hand. He knows your trudging through this great wilderness. These forty years the Lord your God has been with you; you have lacked nothing." ' (Deuteronomy 2:7)*

SCRIPTURE READINGS:

- Deuteronomy 1
- Deuteronomy 2
- Deuteronomy 4:1-14

Questions? Learnings? Praises? Prayers? To Do's? Jesus is…?

DATE:

84
REFLECTION AND PRAYER

Look Back at Last Week — List what God did and what God taught you over the last week. This is your "thank God list" for next week.

Look Forward to Next Week — List what events, decisions, deadlines, or progress needs to happen in the next week. This is your prayer list for next week.

DATE:

THE SHEMA AND #1 COMMANDMENT — GOD IS ONE, LOVE GOD, AND KEEP GOD'S COMMANDMENTS

The Hebrew word "shema" means "hear." Are you hearing God? God is one; totally unique; and God loves you. Are you hearing God? Jesus said the greatest commandment is to love God with all your heart, soul, mind, and strength. We love God because He loves us. Are you hearing God? Jesus said God's love in you changes you, drawing you to a life of keeping His words.

85 READING

> Jesus answered him, "The first of all the commandments is: 'Hear, O Israel, the Lord our God, the Lord is one. And you shall love the Lord your God with all your heart, with all your soul, with all your mind, and with all your strength.' This is the first commandment. (Mark 12:29–30)

SCRIPTURE READINGS:

- Deuteronomy 6:1-5
- Mark 12:28-34
- John 14:21-24

Questions? Learnings? Praises? Prayers? To Do's? Jesus is…?

DATE:

READING 86

HOW TO RAISE CHILDREN — PARENTS SHOULD OBEY THE WORD AND TEACH THE WORD

What does God say is the most important thing parents do for their kids? They show their kids how to love God. When parents love God more than anything, kids see. When parents treasure God's words in their heart, kids know. When parents talk about God like He's the love and joy of their life, kids hear. Godly parents pray constantly that their kids love Jesus the most too.

and that from childhood you have known the Holy Scriptures, which are able to make you wise for salvation through faith which is in Christ Jesus. All Scripture is given by inspiration of God, and is profitable for doctrine, for reproof, for correction, for instruction in righteousness, (2 Timothy 3:15–16)

SCRIPTURE READINGS:

- Deuteronomy 6:6-25
- Deuteronomy 11
- 2 Timothy 3:14-17

Questions? Learnings? Praises? Prayers? To Do's? Jesus is...?

DATE:

THE STORY OF THEIR REBELLIONS — REVIEWING ISRAEL'S REBELLIONS AND GOD'S REDEMPTION

As Moses told the new generation Israel's story, one thing became clear: God was blessing Israel in spite of themselves. Over and over Israel was stubborn and rebellious and forgot God. Why was God blessing them? Because of Him. Because God is love. That's true for you. Jesus blesses you because of Him not you. Jesus' grace is unilateral, unconditional, and beautiful.

87 READING

> *It is not because of your righteousness or the uprightness of your heart that you go in to possess their land, but because of the wickedness of these nations that the Lord your God drives them out from before you, and that He may fulfill the word which the Lord swore to your fathers, to Abraham, Isaac, and Jacob. (Deuteronomy 9:5)*

SCRIPTURE READINGS:

- Deuteronomy 9
- Deuteronomy 10
- Psalms 78:40-59

Questions? Learnings? Praises? Prayers? To Do's? Jesus is...?

DATE:

88 READING

JOSHUA'S CALLING — GOD CALLS JOSHUA TO LEAD AND PROMISES TO NEVER LEAVE HIM

Joshua faced the daunting task of trying to replace Moses. Joshua needed courage to believe what was true: God was with him, God wouldn't leave him, and God would help him every step of the way. What about you? God promised to never leave you or forsake you. How would God change you if you believed that? You'd have more confidence, contentment, joy, and peace.

> Then Moses called Joshua... "Be strong and of good courage, for you must go with this people to the land which the Lord has sworn to their fathers to give them, and you shall cause them to inherit it. And the Lord, He is the One who goes before you. He will be with you, He will not leave you nor forsake you; do not fear nor be dismayed." (Deuteronomy 31:7–8)

SCRIPTURE READINGS:

- Deuteronomy 31
- Deuteronomy 32
- Hebrews 13:5-6

Questions? Learnings? Praises? Prayers? To Do's? Jesus is...?

DATE:

MOSES' DEATH — MOSES' DEATH, HIS DEAD BODY, AND DISCUSSION WITH JESUS ABOUT THE CROSS

Moses' anger cost him the Promised Land. Before Moses died, God graciously showed him the land. Did you know God is gracious to you even when you fail? Moses' body played an interesting role. An angel argued with the devil over his body. Later Jesus taught Moses and Elijah about His death. Perhaps God plans to use Moses again in the end times (Revelation 11).

READING 89

> Then the Lord said to him, "This is the land of which I swore to give Abraham, Isaac, and Jacob, saying, 'I will give it to your descendants.' I have caused you to see it with your eyes, but you shall not cross over there." (Deuteronomy 34:4)

SCRIPTURE READINGS:

- Deuteronomy 34
- Luke 9:27-36
- Jude 9

Questions? Learnings? Praises? Prayers? To Do's? Jesus is...?

DATE:

90 READING

JOSHUA AND HIS CHARGE — BEING STRONG AND COURAGEOUS TO KEEP THE WORD

God gave His people laws and statutes to bless them not restrict them. God's Word revealed the path where His people would find Him and find life. "Do not turn from it to the right hand or to the left." Jesus said He is that path. "I am the way." Jesus is your path to success, joy, and life. Are you living in the path outlined by God's word where you're finding Jesus, His life, and His joy?

> *This Book of the Law shall not depart from your mouth, but you shall meditate in it day and night, that you may observe to do according to all that is written in it. For then you will make your way prosperous, and then you will have good success. (Joshua 1:8)*

SCRIPTURE READINGS:

- Joshua 1
- Deuteronomy 5:28-33
- Psalms 27

Questions? Learnings? Praises? Prayers? To Do's? Jesus is...?

DATE:

91
REFLECTION AND PRAYER

Look Back at Last Week — List what God did and what God taught you over the last week. This is your "thank God list" for next week.

Look Forward to Next Week — List what events, decisions, deadlines, or progress needs to happen in the next week. This is your prayer list for next week.

DATE:

92 READING

RAHAB AND THE SPIES — RAHAB'S FAITH AT WORK AND INCLUSION IN THE GENEALOGY OF CHRIST

Joshua sent two men to spy out Jericho. The city was terrified but the prostitute Rahab believed. Hebrews 11 shows she was saved by faith. James 2 says she was justified by works: hiding the spies showed her faith. Matthew 1 notes she married an Israelite and became an ancestor of Jesus. Rahab's story is your story. Have you, like Rahab, received God's unearned grace?

and [Rahab] said to the men: "I know that the Lord has given you the land, that the terror of you has fallen on us, and that all the inhabitants of the land are fainthearted because of you... for the Lord your God, He is God in heaven above and on earth beneath. (Joshua 2:9, 11)

SCRIPTURE READINGS:

- Joshua 2
- James 2:25-26
- Matthew 1:1-5

Questions? Learnings? Praises? Prayers? To Do's? Jesus is...?

DATE:

JOSHUA AND CROSSING THE JORDAN — JOSHUA'S MIRACLE AND THE MEMORIAL STONES

God didn't stop the waters of the Jordan River until Israel stepped out in faith. Once the priests' feet hit the water, God stopped the river and dried the riverbed. That's what faith is. Faith isn't waiting to move until God moves. Faith is taking a step before God moves because you trust Jesus and His promises. Are you living by faith? Or is there a step God wants you to take?

93 READING

> *And it shall come to pass, as soon as the soles of the feet of the priests who bear the ark of the Lord, the Lord of all the earth, shall rest in the waters of the Jordan, that the waters of the Jordan shall be cut off, the waters that come down from upstream, and they shall stand as a heap." (Joshua 3:13)*

SCRIPTURE READINGS:

- Joshua 3
- Joshua 4
- Psalms 114

Questions? Learnings? Praises? Prayers? To Do's? Jesus is...?

DATE:

94 READING

JOSHUA AND THE COMMANDER — THE COMMANDER OF THE LORD APPEARS AND JESUS WORTHY OF WORSHIP

As Joshua's army recovered from circumcision, a Man with a sword appeared. He said, "I'm not on your side. I'm here to lead." Joshua fell at His feet. The Man was Jesus. When John the apostle bowed down to an angel, the angel said, "Only bow to God." But Joshua met Jesus. Pause right now and pray what Joshua prayed. "What do you say to Your servant?" Then listen.

> ...a Man stood opposite him [Joshua] with His sword drawn in His hand. And Joshua... said... "Are You for us or for our adversaries?" So He said, "No, but as Commander of the army of the Lord I have now come." And Joshua fell on his face to the earth and worshiped, and said to Him, "What does my Lord say to His servant?" (Joshua 5:13-14)

SCRIPTURE READINGS:

- Joshua 5
- Exodus 23:20-23
- Revelation 22:8-9

Questions? Learnings? Praises? Prayers? To Do's? Jesus is...?

DATE:

JOSHUA AND JERICHO — THE FAITH OF JOSHUA/ISRAEL/RAHAB AND OUR SPIRITUAL WARFARE

God promised, "See, I gave Jericho [a stronghold] into your hand." Joshua saw it by faith. Israel marched six days around the stronghold with no progress. Israel marched by faith. On day seven, they marched, shouted, and God tore its walls down. Strongholds pictured things that strongly oppose Jesus being first in your mind and heart. What are the strongholds in your life?

For the weapons of our [spiritual] warfare are not carnal but mighty in God for pulling down strongholds, (2 Corinthians 10:4)

SCRIPTURE READINGS:

- Joshua 6
- Hebrews 11:30-31
- 2 Corinthians 10:3-4

Questions? Learnings? Praises? Prayers? To Do's? Jesus is…?

DATE:

96 READING

JOSHUA AND ACHAN/AI — ONE MAN'S SIN AFFECTS MANY INNOCENT PEOPLE

God said the treasure from the first city, Jericho, was His. God gets the first part of everything we receive. Achan sinned by stealing what was God's and hiding it in his tent. People often try to hide their sins. They think, "It's not hurting anyone." Achan's sin led to 36 innocent deaths. What should you do when you sin? Confess your sin to Jesus. He will forgive you (1 John 1:9).

> *Now Joshua said to Achan, "My son, I beg you, give glory to the Lord God of Israel, and make confession to Him, and tell me now what you have done; do not hide it from me." (Joshua 7:19)*

SCRIPTURE READINGS:

- Joshua 7
- Joshua 8
- Joshua 22:20

Questions? Learnings? Praises? Prayers? To Do's? Jesus is...?

DATE:

JOSHUA AND THE GIBEONITES — ISRAEL'S GULLIBILITY AND NOT ASKING FOR GOD'S COUNSEL

Israel was a few miles from Gibeon but the Gibeonites pretended to be from a far country. How was Israel deceived? They didn't pray to God for wisdom, didn't ask Gibeon enough questions, and didn't wait long enough before committing. Jesus told us, "Do not be deceived." What situations are you asking Jesus about right now? Are you giving God the time to guide you?

97 READING

Then the men of Israel took some of their provisions; but they did not ask counsel of the Lord. (Joshua 9:14)

SCRIPTURE READINGS:

- Joshua 9
- 2 Samuel 21:1-14
- Isaiah 30:1

Questions? Learnings? Praises? Prayers? To Do's? Jesus is...?

DATE:

98
REFLECTION AND PRAYER

Look Back at Last Week — List what God did and what God taught you over the last week. This is your "thank God list" for next week.

Look Forward to Next Week — List what events, decisions, deadlines, or progress needs to happen in the next week. This is your prayer list for next week.

DATE:

JOSHUA AND THE SUN/CONQUESTS — ISRAEL'S ENEMIES AND GOD'S VICTORIES

Joshua led Israel into the center of the land. The enemies of the south attacked them then the north. Joshua defeated them all. Joshua pictured Jesus. Joshua and Jesus are the same name (in Hebrew and Greek). Like Joshua, Jesus leads you, protects you, prays for you, and fights for you. Jesus is your Joshua. Reading the book of Joshua is like reading about life with Jesus.

99 READING

And there has been no day like that, before it or after it, that the Lord heeded the voice of a man; for the Lord fought for Israel. (Joshua 10:14)

SCRIPTURE READINGS:

- Joshua 10
- Joshua 11
- Habakkuk 3:8-14

Questions? Learnings? Praises? Prayers? To Do's? Jesus is...?

DATE:

100 READING

JOSHUA AND DIVIDING THE LAND — SOME TRIBES POSSESS THEIR LAND AND SOME PROCRASTINATE

After the battles, two and a half tribes returned to land they inherited east of the Jordan River. Now it was time for the other tribes to discover where God wanted them to live. Two and a half tribes acted while seven procrastinated. Joshua gathered the seven and said, "Why are you procrastinating? Let's go." Jesus is your Joshua. What are you procrastinating about right now?

Then Joshua said to the children of Israel: "How long will you neglect to go and possess the land which the Lord God of your fathers has given you? (Joshua 18:3)

SCRIPTURE READINGS:

- Joshua 13:1-14
- Joshua 14
- Joshua 18:1-10

Questions? Learnings? Praises? Prayers? To Do's? Jesus is...?

DATE:

JOSHUA'S CHARGE AND DEATH — JOSHUA'S WARNING ABOUT SERVING TWO MASTERS

Joshua saw that Israel wanted to serve God while keeping all their idols. Joshua begged, "Get rid of your idols. You can't serve both." Israel replied, "Don't worry. We promise to just serve God." Back and forth they went. You face the same battle. Jesus said, "You cannot serve God and money." You'll have to choose one. Are you trying to serve Jesus and something else too?

No one can serve two masters; for either he will hate the one and love the other, or else he will be loyal to the one and despise the other. You cannot serve God and mammon [money]. (Matthew 6:24)

SCRIPTURE READINGS:

- Joshua 24
- 1 Samuel 7:2-4
- Matthew 6:24

Questions? Learnings? Praises? Prayers? To Do's? Jesus is...?

DATE:

102 READING

JUDGES ORIGIN — THE DAYS OF THE JUDGES AND THE CYCLE OF SIN/JUDGMENT/PRAYER/DELIVERANCE

The book of Judges recorded the vicious cycle of sin. (1) Israel served God. (2) The leader died. (3) Israel fell away. (4) Enemies enslaved them. (5) Israel cried out. (6) God raised a new judge to deliver. Rinse, lather, repeat. Jesus is your Deliverer that will never die. Cry out to Him. The last verse of the book explains why it can be confusing: everyone did right in their own eyes.

And it came to pass, when the judge was dead, that they reverted and behaved more corruptly than their fathers, by following other gods, to serve them and bow down to them. They did not cease from their own doings nor from their stubborn way. (Judges 2:19)

SCRIPTURE READINGS:

- Judges 1
- Judges 2
- Judges 21:25

Questions? Learnings? Praises? Prayers? To Do's? Jesus is...?

DATE:

JUDGES OTHNIEL, EHUD, AND SHAMGAR — THE CYCLE OF SIN, JUDGMENT, PRAYER, AND DELIVERANCE

The book of Judges recorded the hopeful cycle of deliverance. (1) Trouble. (2) Prayer. (3) Rescue. (4) Glorify God. The book lists 12 judges God raised up to deliver an area of Israel. All 12 judges pictured Jesus. "Othniel" means "lion of God"; Jesus is the Lion of God. Ehud had a two-edged blade; Jesus wields the Bible, a two-edged sword. You are reading about Jesus.

> *And they [nations] were left, that He might test Israel by them, to know whether they would obey the commandments of the Lord, which He had commanded their fathers by the hand of Moses... But when the children of Israel cried out to the Lord, the Lord raised up a deliverer for them... (Judges 3:4, 15)*

SCRIPTURE READINGS:

- Judges 3
- Isaiah 59:12-18
- Psalms 50:15

Questions? Learnings? Praises? Prayers? To Do's? Jesus is...?

DATE:

104 READING

JUDGES DEBORAH AND BARAK — DEBORAH'S FAITH, BARAK'S FAITH, AND GOD'S VICTORY

Barak led 10,000 to defeat Sisera's army and was listed in the "hall of faith" of Hebrews 11. But Barak needed Deborah and Jael. Deborah urged Barak to deploy his army by faith then attack by faith. God used Jael to coax Sisera to sleep and end his life. Jesus created us to need each other. You need others and are needed by others. When we work together, Jesus is glorified.

> *And what more shall I say? For the time would fail me to tell of Gideon and Barak and Samson and Jephthah, also of David and Samuel and the prophets: who through faith subdued kingdoms, worked righteousness, obtained promises, stopped the mouths of lions, (Hebrews 11:32–33)*

SCRIPTURE READINGS:

- Judges 4
- Judges 5
- Hebrews 11:32-34

Questions? Learnings? Praises? Prayers? To Do's? Jesus is…?

DATE:

105
REFLECTION AND PRAYER

Look Back at Last Week — List what God did and what God taught you over the last week. This is your "thank God list" for next week.

Look Forward to Next Week — List what events, decisions, deadlines, or progress needs to happen in the next week. This is your prayer list for next week.

DATE:

106 READING

JUDGE GIDEON — GOD REDUCES GIDEON'S ARMY TO ENSURE GOD GETS ALL THE CREDIT

Gideon's 32,000 faced 135,000 Midianites (Judges 8:10). Gideon had too many. He was only outnumbered 4.2 to 1. God shrunk them to 10,000. They were still too strong, outnumbered 13.5 to 1. God shrunk them to 300. Being outnumbered 450 to 1 was perfect. No one would take God's glory. Gideon pictures Jesus for you. Jesus chooses the weak so He gets all the glory.

And the Lord said to Gideon, "The people who are with you are too many for Me to give the Midianites into their hands, lest Israel claim glory for itself against Me, saying, 'My own hand has saved me.' (Judges 7:2)

SCRIPTURE READINGS:

- Judges 6
- Judges 7
- 1 Corinthians 1:26-31

Questions? Learnings? Praises? Prayers? To Do's? Jesus is...?

DATE:

JUDGE SAMSON — THE NAZIRITE VOW TO SEPARATE YOURSELF TO THE LORD

When God prompted an Israelite to serve Him, they would take the vow of a Nazirite. Nazirites separated themselves from wine, grapes, and haircuts to devote themselves to God. Samson was a Nazirite from birth, separated to be a judge and deliverer. Samson sometimes pictures Jesus for you too: called from birth, separate from the world, strong, and filled with the Spirit.

107 READING

Speak to the children of Israel, and say to them: 'When either a man or woman consecrates an offering to take the vow of a Nazirite, to separate himself to the Lord... All the days of his separation he shall be holy to the Lord. (Numbers 6:2, 8)

SCRIPTURE READINGS:

- Judges 13
- Numbers 6:1-21
- Amos 2:10-13

Questions? Learnings? Praises? Prayers? To Do's? Jesus is...?

DATE:

108 READING

JUDGE SAMSON — SAMSON, THE SPIRIT, AND VICTORY WITH THE JAWBONE OF A DONKEY

What was the key to Samson's strength? Not his muscles. Nor his hair (uncut as a Nazirite). It was the Holy Spirit. Over and over, we read, "the Spirit of the LORD came mightily upon him." What are your strengths? Natural intelligence? Good planning? Hard work? Common sense? If you're a Christian, Jesus' Spirit lives in you. Strength isn't about might or power. It's about Him.

So he answered and said to me: "This is the word of the Lord to Zerubbabel: 'Not by might nor by power, but by My Spirit,' Says the Lord of hosts. (Zechariah 4:6)

SCRIPTURE READINGS:

- Judges 14
- Judges 15
- Zechariah 4:6

Questions? Learnings? Praises? Prayers? To Do's? Jesus is...?

DATE:

JUDGE SAMSON — DELILAH'S NAGGING, SAMSON'S FOOLISHNESS, AND SAMSON'S DEATH

Samson loved women who didn't follow God. Delilah was paid to find the source of Samson's strength. Day after day, Delilah wore him down and Samson got closer to the truth. Tie me up. Use new ropes. Weave my hair. Cut my hair. Samson's temptation pictured the daily temptation you face to give yourself to people or things who break your connection with Jesus.

109
READING

And it came to pass, when she pestered him daily with her words and pressed him, so that his soul was vexed to death, that he told her all his heart... "If I am shaven, then my strength will leave me, and I shall become weak, and be like any other man." (Judges 16:16–17)

SCRIPTURE READINGS:

- Judges 16
- Proverbs 5:1-14
- Proverbs 27:15-16

Questions? Learnings? Praises? Prayers? To Do's? Jesus is...?

DATE:

110 READING

RUTH FOLLOWS NAOMI — THE STORY OF THE MOABITES AND GOD'S LOVE FOR FOREIGNERS/WIDOWS

Elimelech and Naomi moved to Moab because of famine. Their sons married Moabites. Then Elimelech and his sons died leaving behind three widows. When Naomi moved home, one woman left and one stayed: her name was Ruth. Ruth pictures a Christian: born outside of God's family; then meeting people who walk with Jesus; then drawn to make Jesus their Savior and God.

> *But Ruth said: "Entreat me not to leave you, Or to turn back from following after you; For wherever you go, I will go; And wherever you lodge, I will lodge; Your people shall be my people, And your God, my God. Where you die, I will die, And there will I be buried. The Lord do so to me, and more also, If anything but death parts you and me." (Ruth 1:16–17)*

SCRIPTURE READINGS:

- Ruth 1
- Deuteronomy 23:3-6
- Deuteronomy 10:17-19

Questions? Learnings? Praises? Prayers? To Do's? Jesus is…?

DATE:

RUTH MEETS BOAZ — CARING FOR THE POOR AND ALLOWING THE POOR TO COLLECT FOOD AFTER HARVEST

Naomi and Ruth moved back to Israel during harvest. Ruth went to gather food for her family. God loves foreigners and cares for the poor. Ruth was both. Do you love foreigners and care for the poor like Jesus does? Boaz owned the field where Ruth gathered. Boaz watched Ruth, asked about her, protected her, and blessed her. What Boaz did for Ruth, Jesus does for you.

111

READING

And Boaz answered and said to her, "It has been fully reported to me, all that you have done for your mother-in-law since the death of your husband, and how you have left your father and your mother and the land of your birth, and have come to a people whom you did not know before. 12 The Lord repay your work, and a full reward be given you by the Lord..." (Ruth 2:11–12)

SCRIPTURE READINGS:

- Ruth 2
- Deuteronomy 15:7-11
- Deuteronomy 24:17-22

Questions? Learnings? Praises? Prayers? To Do's? Jesus is...?

DATE:

112
REFLECTION AND PRAYER

Look Back at Last Week — List what God did and what God taught you over the last week. This is your "thank God list" for next week.

Look Forward to Next Week — List what events, decisions, deadlines, or progress needs to happen in the next week. This is your prayer list for next week.

DATE:

RUTH'S VIRTUE — THE LAW OF THE KINSMAN REDEEMER AND RUTH THE VIRTUOUS WOMAN

Naomi saw God at work. Ruth gathered food in the field of Boaz who was related to her deceased husband. God provided for widows through the law of the "kinsman redeemer." If a man died without a son, the closest male relative married the widow. Naomi told Ruth to find out if Boaz would marry her. Do you see Jesus at work when others don't realize it? He is at work. He is redeeming.

113

READING

Then she said, "Sit still, my daughter, until you know how the matter will turn out; for the man will not rest until he has concluded the matter this day." (Ruth 3:18)

SCRIPTURE READINGS:

- Ruth 3
- Deuteronomy 25:5-10
- Proverbs 31:10-31

Questions? Learnings? Praises? Prayers? To Do's? Jesus is...?

DATE:

READING 114

RUTH'S REDEMPTION — THE LAW OF THE KINSMAN REDEEMER AND THE GENEALOGY OF JESUS

Boaz brought another possible "kinsman redeemer" for Ruth to the authorities. When he couldn't marry Ruth, Boaz did. Ruth became his wife, the great-grandmother of David, and ancestor of Jesus. If you're a Christian, Boaz pictures Jesus. Jesus pursued you. No other redeemer could help you. So Jesus redeemed you. Now you're a part of the bride of Christ.

So Boaz took Ruth and she became his wife; and when he went in to her, the Lord gave her conception, and she bore a son. Then the women said to Naomi, "Blessed be the Lord, who has not left you this day without a close relative; and may his name be famous in Israel! (Ruth 4:13–14)

SCRIPTURE READINGS:

- Ruth 4
- Matthew 22:23-33
- Matthew 1:1-6

Questions? Learnings? Praises? Prayers? To Do's? Jesus is…?

DATE:

HANNAH'S PRAYER — HANNAH'S PROBLEM, PRAYER, PEACE, AND THANKFULNESS FOR BABY SAMUEL

Elkanah married Hannah and Peninnah. Hannah desperately wanted a baby. Peninnah had kids and tormented Hannah with it. Hannah wept and prayed until her prayer changed. Instead of praying for herself, she prayed for a child she would give back to God. God answered. Jesus doesn't want you to be anxious. Let Jesus know your requests and He will give you His peace.

115 READING

> *Then they rose early in the morning and worshiped before the Lord, and returned and came to their house at Ramah. And Elkanah knew Hannah his wife, and the Lord remembered her. So it came to pass in the process of time that Hannah conceived and bore a son, and called his name Samuel, saying, "Because I have asked for him from the Lord." (1 Samuel 1:19–20)*

SCRIPTURE READINGS:

- 1 Samuel 1
- 1 Samuel 2:1-11
- Philippians 4:6-7

Questions? Learnings? Praises? Prayers? To Do's? Jesus is...?

DATE:

116 READING

SAMUEL'S CALL — THE WICKEDNESS OF ELI'S SONS AND SAMUEL'S CALL FROM GOD

The child Samuel didn't know how to recognize God's voice. "Samuel, Samuel." He thought it was Eli. Eli taught Samuel that he was actually hearing God. "When you hear God, tell Him you're listening." If you're a Christian, Jesus speaks to you from inside you. Are you like Samuel, not yet realizing that some of your thoughts aren't yours? It's Jesus speaking to you.

> And the Lord called Samuel again the third time. So he arose and went to Eli, and said, "Here I am, for you did call me." Then Eli perceived that the Lord had called the boy. Therefore Eli said to Samuel, "Go, lie down; and it shall be, if He calls you, that you must say, 'Speak, Lord, for Your servant hears.'" So Samuel went and lay down in his place. (1 Samuel 3:8–9)

SCRIPTURE READINGS:

- 1 Samuel 2:12-21
- 1 Samuel 3
- Psalms 99:6-7

Questions? Learnings? Praises? Prayers? To Do's? Jesus is…?

DATE:

GOD'S JUDGMENT — ISRAEL IS DEFEATED, ELI AND HIS SONS DIE, AND THE ARK IS LOST

Eli's sons were now priests. They were religious leaders who stole from God and slept with women. Sadly, Eli chose to honor his kids more than God. Do you care more about someone than Jesus? The ark pictured God's presence with Israel but Israel had departed from God. God let the ark be captured to show everyone that the glory of God had departed from His people.

Why do you [Eli] kick at My sacrifice and My offering which I have commanded in My dwelling place, and honor your sons more than Me, to make yourselves fat with the best of all the offerings of Israel My people?' (1 Samuel 2:29)

SCRIPTURE READINGS:

- 1 Samuel 2:22-36
- 1 Samuel 4
- 1 Kings 2:26-27

Questions? Learnings? Praises? Prayers? To Do's? Jesus is...?

117 READING

DATE:

118 READING

THE ARK IS RETURNED — GOD JUDGES THE PHILISTINES, THEIR IDOL DAGON, AND ALL FALSE IDOLS

The Philistines put the ark in Dagon's temple. Dagon was an idol, a lifeless statue. The next morning, the Philistines found their idol on its face before the ark. The ark pictured Jesus. In your life, an idol is anything more important to you than Jesus. Are your friends your idol? Are your kids your idol? Have you made an idol of money, career, sports, sex, food, vacations, etc.?

> *But our God is in heaven; He does whatever He pleases. Their idols are silver and gold, The work of men's hands. (Psalm 115:3–4)*

SCRIPTURE READINGS:

- 1 Samuel 5
- 1 Samuel 6
- Psalms 115:3-8

Questions? Learnings? Praises? Prayers? To Do's? Jesus is...?

DATE:

119
REFLECTION AND PRAYER

Look Back at Last Week — List what God did and what God taught you over the last week. This is your "thank God list" for next week.

Look Forward to Next Week — List what events, decisions, deadlines, or progress needs to happen in the next week. This is your prayer list for next week.

DATE:

120 READING

ISRAEL WANTS A KING — ISRAEL REJECTS GOD AS THEIR KING

Israel wanted a king to be like all the other nations. In what ways are you tempted, like Israel, to be like everyone else? Israel already had God as their King. God warned Israel about what human kings would do to them. They wanted one anyway. If you're a Christian, Jesus is your King. He's the King of Kings. In what ways are you looking to Jesus to lead you as King?

> *Then all the elders of Israel gathered together and came to Samuel at Ramah, and said to him, "Look, you are old, and your sons do not walk in your ways. Now make us a king to judge us like all the nations." (1 Samuel 8:4-5)*

SCRIPTURE READINGS:

- 1 Samuel 7
- 1 Samuel 8
- Hosea 13:9-11

Questions? Learnings? Praises? Prayers? To Do's? Jesus is...?

DATE:

SAUL ANOINTED AS KING — KING SAUL AND GOD'S LAWS FOR A KING

When Israel rejected God as King, they received Saul, a tall and handsome man who wasn't faithful to God. God warned kings not to multiply horses, wives, or gold (i.e. sins of power, sex, or greed). God promised to protect kings as they read the Bible daily. Today Jesus makes every Christian a king (Revelation 1:6). Are you letting Jesus transform you through the Bible too?

121 READING

> Also it shall be, when he sits on the throne of his kingdom, that he shall write for himself a copy of this law in a book, from the one before the priests, the Levites. And it shall be with him, and he shall read it all the days of his life, that he may learn to fear the Lord his God and be careful to observe all the words of this law and these statutes, (Deuteronomy 17:18-19)

SCRIPTURE READINGS:

- 1 Samuel 9
- 1 Samuel 10
- Deuteronomy 17:14-20

Questions? Learnings? Praises? Prayers? To Do's? Jesus is…?

DATE:

122 READING

SAUL OBEYS GOD — SAUL'S CORONATION, SAMUEL'S PRAYER, AND PRAYING FOR THE GOVERNMENT

At King Saul's coronation, Samuel reminded Israel how God loved them over the years but they wanted another to be king. Israel begged Samuel to pray for them. Samuel promised to never stop praying. Samuel pictured Jesus who never stops praying and interceding for you. If Christ is living inside you, He prompts you to pray for people too. Who is He moving you to pray for?

Moreover, as for me, far be it from me that I should sin against the Lord in ceasing to pray for you; but I will teach you the good and the right way. (1 Samuel 12:23)

SCRIPTURE READINGS:

- 1 Samuel 11
- 1 Samuel 12
- 1 Timothy 2:1-2

Questions? Learnings? Praises? Prayers? To Do's? Jesus is...?

DATE:

SAUL DISOBEYS — SAUL'S UNLAWFUL SACRIFICE, SPARING AGAG, AND DAVID'S HEART FOR GOD

Saul disobeyed God by not waiting for Samuel to offer a sacrifice (only priests could offer it). Saul disobeyed God by sparing King Agag and the best animals (God said to destroy all). So God sought for a king after His heart. Jesus wants your heart. Do you love Jesus so much that, unlike Saul, you trust Him enough to wait for Him? Do you believe Him enough to obey Him?

> *And when He had removed him [King Saul], He raised up for them David as king, to whom also He gave testimony and said, 'I have found David the son of Jesse, a man after My own heart, who will do all My will.' (Acts 13:22)*

SCRIPTURE READINGS:

- 1 Samuel 13:1-15
- 1 Samuel 15
- Acts 13:16-23

Questions? Learnings? Praises? Prayers? To Do's? Jesus is...?

DATE:

124 READING

JONATHAN'S VICTORY — JONATHAN'S FAITH IN GOD'S ABILITY TO HELP THOSE WITHOUT POWER

Saul and Jonathan had swords. Their army had gardening tools. Facing a Philistine army across a valley, Jonathan said to His armor bearer, "Maybe God will use us. God can save with many or few." When they attacked, God created confusion and Israel won. Jesus is not limited by your weakness or lack of resources. In fact, Jesus gets more glory when it's clear He won the victory.

And Asa cried out to the Lord his God, and said, "Lord, it is nothing for You to help, whether with many or with those who have no power; help us, O Lord our God, for we rest on You, and in Your name we go against this multitude. O Lord, You are our God; do not let man prevail against You!" (2 Chronicles 14:11)

SCRIPTURE READINGS:

- 1 Samuel 13:16-23
- 1 Samuel 14
- 2 Chronicles 14:11

Questions? Learnings? Praises? Prayers? To Do's? Jesus is...?

DATE:

DAVID ANOINTED AS KING — GOD'S CHOOSES DAVID AND SAYS NOT TO JUDGE BY APPEARANCE

Samuel saw Jesse's oldest son Eliab and said, "This has to be the next king." God warned Samuel not to judge someone based on how they look. God looks at the heart of people. David's heart was full of faith, humility, and love for God. Jesus warned us about the same thing. "Do not judge according to appearance." Do you focus on how people look or their heart?

> But the Lord said to Samuel, "Do not look at his appearance or at his physical stature, because I have refused him. For the Lord does not see as man sees; for man looks at the outward appearance, but the Lord looks at the heart." (1 Samuel 16:7)

SCRIPTURE READINGS:

- 1 Samuel 16
- Psalms 78:70-72
- John 7:24

Questions? Learnings? Praises? Prayers? To Do's? Jesus is...?

DATE:

126
REFLECTION AND PRAYER

Look Back at Last Week — List what God did and what God taught you over the last week. This is your "thank God list" for next week.

Look Forward to Next Week — List what events, decisions, deadlines, or progress needs to happen in the next week. This is your prayer list for next week.

DATE:

DAVID AND GOLIATH — DAVID THE SHEPHERD VS. THE GIANT GOLIATH (WHO HAS FOUR RELATIVES)

The giant Goliath cursed God and called to Israel for a challenger. David knew Goliath was big but God was bigger. Are you facing big problems? Jesus is bigger than your problems. David took five smooth stones. (Goliath did have four relatives.) David's victory pictured Jesus' victory at the cross. Both were shepherds who defeated a mighty enemy and saved their people's lives.

127 READING

Yea, though I walk through the valley of the shadow of death, I will fear no evil; For You are with me; Your rod and Your staff, they comfort me. (Psalm 23:4)

SCRIPTURE READINGS:

- 1 Samuel 17
- Psalms 23
- 2 Samuel 21:15-22

Questions? Learnings? Praises? Prayers? To Do's? Jesus is…?

DATE:

128 READING

SAUL'S INSECURITY — KING SAUL IS JEALOUS OF DAVID, FEARS DAVID, AND MANIPULATES DAVID

Envy is like cancer. It starts with a single cancerous thought. "Why don't I have that?" Left to itself, it spreads. Saul's attitude turned cancerous when he heard people sing, "David killed ten thousands." Envy is the opposite of love; the opposite of Jesus. When you love, you want good things for others. Is Jesus filling your heart with love for others instead of envying them?

A sound heart is life to the body, But envy is rottenness to the bones. (Proverbs 14:30)

SCRIPTURE READINGS:

- 1 Samuel 18
- Proverbs 14:30
- James 3:13-16

Questions? Learnings? Praises? Prayers? To Do's? Jesus is...?

DATE:

SAUL ATTACKS DAVID — SAUL'S ANGER WITH DAVID AND DAVID'S ESCAPE FROM SAUL

Saul wanted David dead. He tried to spear him twice and tried to capture him at home. David wrote Psalm 59 after his wife helped him escape through a window. David wasn't fighting Saul. He was fighting to trust God. Have you ever felt attacked? Your battle, like David's, isn't against people (Ephesians 6:12). Your battle is to trust that Jesus really loves you and is protecting you.

Whenever I am afraid, I will trust in You. In God (I will praise His word), In God I have put my trust; I will not fear. What can flesh do to me? (Psalm 56:3–4)

SCRIPTURE READINGS:

- 1 Samuel 19
- Psalms 59
- Psalms 56:3-6

Questions? Learnings? Praises? Prayers? To Do's? Jesus is…?

DATE:

130 READING

JONATHAN HELPS DAVID — THE FRIENDSHIP OF JONATHAN, DAVID, AND JESUS

Friendship is great. Friendship with Jesus at the center (AKA fellowship) is better. Jonathan and David loved and supported each other with God at the center of their friendship. "The LORD be between you and me forever." Jesus created you to experience His joy through fellowship too (1 John 1:3-4). Are you investing in friendships where you both experience Jesus' love and joy?

This is My commandment, that you love one another as I [Jesus] have loved you. (John 15:12)

SCRIPTURE READINGS:

- 1 Samuel 20
- Proverbs 27:4-10
- John 15:12-17

Questions? Learnings? Praises? Prayers? To Do's? Jesus is...?

DATE:

DAVID ON THE RUN — DAVID EATS THE HOLY BREAD AND JESUS COMMENTS TO THE PHARISEES

David ran to the priest Ahimelech who gave him old temple showbreads (which priests ate). Jesus referenced this story when telling the Pharisees they misinterpreted the Bible. Later David ran to Gath, the city of Goliath, and faked madness to escape. David wrote Psalm 34 about God's deliverance. Are you running from something? Run to Jesus instead. He will protect you.

131

READING

The face of the Lord is against those who do evil, To cut off the remembrance of them from the earth. The righteous cry out, and the Lord hears, And delivers them out of all their troubles. (Psalm 34:16–17)

SCRIPTURE READINGS:

- 1 Samuel 21
- Psalms 34
- Matthew 12:1-8

Questions? Learnings? Praises? Prayers? To Do's? Jesus is...?

DATE:

132 READING

DAVID IN THE CAVE — DAVID RUNS TO A CAVE, PRAYS TO GOD, AND WRITES PSALMS

In desperation, David fled to a cave. Have you isolated yourself to solve your problems? In the dark, David poured out his heart in Psalm 142. He told God the cave wasn't helping. "You are my refuge." He wrote another prayer in the cave which became Psalm 57. David showed you how to write a letter to God and pour out your heart. Try writing a letter to Jesus today.

I pour out my complaint before Him; I declare before Him my trouble. (Psalm 142:2)

SCRIPTURE READINGS:

- 1 Samuel 22:1
- Psalms 142
- Psalms 57

Questions? Learnings? Praises? Prayers? To Do's? Jesus is...?

DATE:

133
REFLECTION AND PRAYER

Look Back at Last Week — List what God did and what God taught you over the last week. This is your "thank God list" for next week.

Look Forward to Next Week — List what events, decisions, deadlines, or progress needs to happen in the next week. This is your prayer list for next week.

DATE:

134 READING

DOEG KILLS PRIESTS — DAVID FLEES TO WILDERNESS, PRIESTS ARE MURDERED, AND DAVID WRITES PSALMS

David wrote Psalm 63 as he hid in the dry wilderness. Physical thirst reminded him of his spiritual thirst for God. God created you with a thirst for Jesus too. Are you trying to quench it with something else? David wrote Psalm 52 as he thought about Ahimelech's murder. He knew God is just and will judge every wicked deed. Are you trusting that Jesus will right every wrong?

> *O God, You are my God; Early will I seek You; My soul thirsts for You; My flesh longs for You In a dry and thirsty land Where there is no water. (Psalm 63:1)*

SCRIPTURE READINGS:

- 1 Samuel 22
- Psalms 63
- Psalms 52

Questions? Learnings? Praises? Prayers? To Do's? Jesus is...?

DATE:

DAVID HIDES AND SPARES SAUL — THE ZIPHITES TELL SAUL WHERE DAVID IS AND DAVID WRITES A PSALM

David's trials prompted him to pray over and over. "Do we attack?" (Yes.) "Are you sure?" (Yes.) "Will Saul come?" (Yes.) "Will this city betray me?" (Yes.) David wrote Psalm 54 after the Ziphites revealed his location to King Saul. "Save me, O God, by Your name." Is Jesus allowing you to face trials right now to help you pray more often with more urgency and transparency?

135
READING

Will the men of Keilah deliver me into his hand? Will Saul come down, as Your servant has heard? O Lord God of Israel, I pray, tell Your servant." And the Lord said, "He will come down." Then David said, "Will the men of Keilah deliver me and my men into the hand of Saul?" And the Lord said, "They will deliver you." (1 Samuel 23:11–12)

SCRIPTURE READINGS:

- 1 Samuel 23
- 1 Samuel 24
- Psalms 54

Questions? Learnings? Praises? Prayers? To Do's? Jesus is...?

DATE:

136 READING

ABIGAIL AND NABAL — NABAL (WHOSE NAME MEANS "FOOL") AND FOOLISHNESS

Nabal was a fool for insulting David who was protecting Nabal's flocks. Nabal literally means "fool." A fool is someone who is arrogant, won't listen, or lives as if God doesn't exist. Do you live in the humility of Jesus? Do you listen? Do you live as if God exists? Nabal's wife Abigail pictured you. Just like David married Abigail, Jesus will marry His beautiful bride, the church.

> *The fool has said in his heart, "There is no God." They are corrupt, They have done abominable works, There is none who does good. (Psalm 14:1)*

SCRIPTURE READINGS:

- 1 Samuel 25
- Psalms 14:1-3
- Proverbs 10:6-25

Questions? Learnings? Praises? Prayers? To Do's? Jesus is...?

DATE:

DAVID SPARES SAUL AGAIN — DAVID SNEAKS INTO SAUL'S CAMP BUT DOES NOT TAKE REVENGE

David had chances to take revenge on Saul but didn't. Once, Saul went to the bathroom where David hid. Later, David snuck up on Saul as he slept. It's natural to want revenge. It's just not Jesus. Jesus loved and died for His enemies (including you). Do you need Jesus to set you free from bitterness? Then love your enemies, do good things for them, and pray God blesses them.

137 READING

But I [Jesus] say to you, love your enemies, bless those who curse you, do good to those who hate you, and pray for those who spitefully use you and persecute you, (Matthew 5:44)

SCRIPTURE READINGS:

- 1 Samuel 26
- Matthew 5:38-48
- Romans 12:14-21

Questions? Learnings? Praises? Prayers? To Do's? Jesus is…?

DATE:

138 READING

SAUL CONSULTS A MEDIUM — GOD IS SILENT TO SAUL AND SAUL TRIES TO CONSULT THE DEAD

Saul banned fortune tellers and psychics then asked a psychic to channel Samuel's spirit. (Psychics don't hear the dead. They hear demons pretending to be the dead.) She shrieked when she saw Samuel. God made an exception to tell Saul he would die. When you need guidance, never consult psychics or "the dead." Pray to Jesus and listen to His Holy Spirit.

So Saul died for his unfaithfulness which he had committed against the Lord, because he did not keep the word of the Lord, and also because he consulted a medium for guidance. (1 Chronicles 10:13)

SCRIPTURE READINGS:

- 1 Samuel 28
- 1 Chronicles 10:13-14
- Proverbs 1:22-33

Questions? Learnings? Praises? Prayers? To Do's? Jesus is...?

DATE:

DAVID CHASES THE AMALEKITES — FINDING STRENGTH IN GOD DURING HARD TIMES

The Philistines didn't let David go with them to the fight against Israel. David was disappointed but didn't know his camp had been raided. Sometimes God says no to guide us to something better. At the camp, David was despondent. Men talked of stoning him. He found strength in the Lord. Jesus wants to use your hard times to show you He has all the strength and joy you need.

139 READING

> *Now David was greatly distressed, for the people spoke of stoning him, because the soul of all the people was grieved, every man for his sons and his daughters. But David strengthened himself in the Lord his God. (1 Samuel 30:6)*

SCRIPTURE READINGS:

- 1 Samuel 29
- 1 Samuel 30
- Habakkuk 3:17-19

Questions? Learnings? Praises? Prayers? To Do's? Jesus is…?

DATE:

140
REFLECTION AND PRAYER

Look Back at Last Week — List what God did and what God taught you over the last week. This is your "thank God list" for next week.

Look Forward to Next Week — List what events, decisions, deadlines, or progress needs to happen in the next week. This is your prayer list for next week.

DATE:

SAUL AND JONATHAN DIE — DAVID MOURNS AND GOD TAKES NO PLEASURE IN THE DEATH OF THE WICKED

When Saul died, David didn't rejoice. He wept. Sometimes when wicked leaders die, people rejoice. God doesn't rejoice. Yes, God is angry with the wicked every day (Psalm 7:11). But God is also patiently giving them time every day to turn back to Him (Romans 2:4). If you're led by Jesus living inside you, you don't rejoice when wicked people die. You mourn for them.

> *Say to them: 'As I live,' says the Lord God, 'I have no pleasure in the death of the wicked, but that the wicked turn from his way and live. Turn, turn from your evil ways! For why should you die, O house of Israel?' (Ezekiel 33:11)*

SCRIPTURE READINGS:

- 1 Chronicles 10
- 2 Samuel 1
- Ezekiel 33:11

Questions? Learnings? Praises? Prayers? To Do's? Jesus is...?

142 READING

ABNER AND ISHBOSHETH DIE — THE MURDERS OF GENERAL ABNER AND KING ISHBOSHETH

Abner's reconciliation with David pictured our reconciliation with Jesus (i.e. salvation). Abner tried to follow a different king. When his king failed him, he made David his king (a picture of salvation). David's kindness to Abner pictured Jesus' kindness to a new Christian: Jesus welcomes you (his former enemy), forgives you, and gives you a new purpose in His kingdom.

> *Then Abner said to David, "I will arise and go, and gather all Israel to my lord the king, that they may make a covenant with you, and that you may reign over all that your heart desires." So David sent Abner away, and he went in peace. (2 Samuel 3:21)*

SCRIPTURE READINGS:

- 2 Samuel 2
- 2 Samuel 3
- 2 Samuel 4

Questions? Learnings? Praises? Prayers? To Do's? Jesus is…?

DATE:

DAVID DEFEATS JERUSALEM AND THE PHILISTINES — DAVID'S BATTLES AND COMMITMENT TO PRAY

David often pictured Jesus. David reigned from Jerusalem (like Jesus will). David was humble about God's blessings (like Jesus is humble). David continually prayed for wisdom (like Jesus continually prays at the right hand of God). One time, the Philistine army gathered. He prayed. When they gathered again, he prayed again. Do you ask again and again for Jesus' guidance?

If any of you lacks wisdom, let him ask of God, who gives to all liberally and without reproach, and it will be given to him. But let him ask in faith, with no doubting, for he who doubts is like a wave of the sea driven and tossed by the wind. (James 1:5-6)

SCRIPTURE READINGS:

- 2 Samuel 5
- 1 Chronicles 11:4-9
- James 1:2-8

Questions? Learnings? Praises? Prayers? To Do's? Jesus is...?

143 READING

DATE:

144 READING

DAVID AND THE ARK — THE ARK, THE DEATH OF UZZAH, AND DAVID'S DANCE

God said to carry the ark on poles but David moved it on a new cart. When the oxen stumbled, Uzzah tried to steady the ark and God struck him down. The ark pictured God's throne: holy; pure; undefiled; impossible to approach in our human sinfulness. Jesus died to make you holy and give you direct access to God's throne (Hebrews 4:14-16). Pause to thank Jesus for that.

> *You have turned for me my mourning into dancing; You have put off my sackcloth and clothed me with gladness, To the end that my glory may sing praise to You and not be silent. O Lord my God, I will give thanks to You forever. (Psalm 30:11–12)*

SCRIPTURE READINGS:

- 2 Samuel 6
- Numbers 4:15-20
- Psalm 30

Questions? Learnings? Praises? Prayers? To Do's? Jesus is…?

DATE:

DAVID AND THE TEMPLE — DAVID PREPARES FOR THE TEMPLE AFTER GOD FORBIDS HIM TO BUILD IT

David wanted to build the Temple because he had a nice house while the ark was in a tent. When David asked for godly counsel, Nathan said, "Do it." Then God told Nathan to tell David no. How do you respond when God tells you no? David responded by thanking God for blessing him then he prepared his son to follow God. That's how Jesus leads you to respond to His no.

> Then King David went in and sat before the Lord; and he said: "Who am I, O Lord God? And what is my house, that You have brought me this far?... So let Your name be magnified forever, saying, 'The Lord of hosts is the God over Israel.' And let the house of Your servant David be established before You. (2 Samuel 7:18, 26)

SCRIPTURE READINGS:

- 2 Samuel 7
- 1 Chronicles 22
- 1 Chronicles 29:1-9

Questions? Learnings? Praises? Prayers? To Do's? Jesus is...?

DATE:

146 READING

DAVID AND HIS WARS — DAVID, THE WARRIOR FOR GOD

David led Israel against the Philistines, Moab, Zobah, Syria, Edom, etc. Israel didn't win because of David. They won because of God. "The Lord preserved David wherever he went." David wrote Psalm 60 and 144 to remember all God did in the fight. The battles you face aren't about you either. They're about Jesus. "The help of man is useless; through God we will win."

> *Give us help from trouble, For the help of man is useless. Through God we will do valiantly, For it is He who shall tread down our enemies. (Psalm 60:11-12)*

SCRIPTURE READINGS:

- 2 Samuel 8
- Psalm 60
- Psalm 144

Questions? Learnings? Praises? Prayers? To Do's? Jesus is...?

DATE:

147

REFLECTION AND PRAYER

Look Back at Last Week — List what God did and what God taught you over the last week. This is your "thank God list" for next week.

Look Forward to Next Week — List what events, decisions, deadlines, or progress needs to happen in the next week. This is your prayer list for next week.

DATE:

148 READING

DAVID AND BATHSHEBA — DAVID'S SIN, CONFESSION, JUDGMENT, AND BIRTH OF SOLOMON

Being bored and alone can be dangerous. One spring, David stayed home from battle, saw Bathsheba, and took her. When she got pregnant, David tried to cover it up by bringing Uriah back from war. Then he killed Uriah. After being caught, David was broken and wrote Psalm 51. When you sin, you can pray Psalm 51 too. Confess it all to Jesus. He will forgive (1 John 1:9).

Wash me thoroughly from my iniquity, And cleanse me from my sin. For I acknowledge my transgressions, And my sin is always before me. (Psalm 51:2-3)

SCRIPTURE READINGS:

- 2 Samuel 11
- 2 Samuel 12:1-25
- Psalm 51

Questions? Learnings? Praises? Prayers? To Do's? Jesus is...?

DATE:

DAVID, AMNON, TAMAR, AND ABSALOM — DAVID, THE PASSIVE FATHER

David's son Amnon sexually assaulted his half-sister Tamar. By the law of Moses, he should die. David did nothing. Two years later, Tamar's brother Absalom killed Amnon. David did nothing. Three years later, Joab orchestrated Absalom's return. David did nothing. David was often a passive father. Jesus is peaceful, not passive. Is He prompting you to end an area of passivity?

149 READING

> *But when King David heard of all these things, he was very angry... And it came to pass, after two full years, that Absalom had sheepshearers in Baal Hazor, which is near Ephraim; so Absalom invited all the king's sons. (2 Samuel 13:21, 23)*

SCRIPTURE READINGS:

- 2 Samuel 13
- 2 Samuel 14
- Deuteronomy 22:25-27

Questions? Learnings? Praises? Prayers? To Do's? Jesus is...?

DATE:

150 READING

ABSALOM'S TREASON — ABSALOM'S INSURRECTION AND DAVID'S ESCAPE

Absalom stole Israel's hearts from his dad then led a coup. David wept as he fled for his life with his family and guard. David wrote Psalm 3 to pour out his sorrow. "You, O LORD, are a shield for me." David was battling to believe God's promises to him. When do you experience Jesus being your shield? When you have no other defense; when you're forced to trust Him alone.

Lord, how they have increased who trouble me! Many are they who rise up against me. Many are they who say of me, "There is no help for him in God." Selah (Psalm 3:1-2)

SCRIPTURE READINGS:

- 2 Samuel 15
- 2 Samuel 17:25-29
- Psalm 3

Questions? Learnings? Praises? Prayers? To Do's? Jesus is...?

DATE:

ABSALOM'S DEATH — ABSALOM'S MURDER AND DAVID'S MOURNING

151 READING

David told his army not to hurt Absalom then defeated his army. Joab found Absalom hanging from a tree (a sign of being cursed, Deuteronomy 21:22-23) and killed him. David wept for his son. How many parents have wept for their kids, saying, "Where did it go wrong?" David wished he died in Absalom's place. Jesus did die in your place. Jesus took your place on the cross.

Then the king was deeply moved, and went up to the chamber over the gate, and wept. And as he went, he said thus: "O my son Absalom—my son, my son Absalom—if only I had died in your place! O Absalom my son, my son!" (2 Samuel 18:33)

SCRIPTURE READINGS:

- 2 Samuel 18
- 2 Samuel 19:1-23
- 2 Samuel 12:9-12

Questions? Learnings? Praises? Prayers? To Do's? Jesus is...?

DATE:

152 READING

DAVID AND THE PSALMS — DAVID, THE SWEET PSALMIST OF ISRAEL, WRITES PSALM 18

When David's battles were over, he wrote psalms to thank God like 2 Samuel 22 (adapted for public worship as Psalm 18). David wrote almost half (73 of 150) of the Psalms, the Jewish hymn book. The Psalms help you process every season with Jesus: joy and sadness; victory and loss; hope and depression. Jesus created you to process your whole life with Him.

> *I will call upon the Lord, who is worthy to be praised; So shall I be saved from my enemies. (2 Samuel 22:4)*

SCRIPTURE READINGS:

- 2 Samuel 22
- 2 Samuel 23:1-7
- Psalm 18

Questions? Learnings? Praises? Prayers? To Do's? Jesus is…?

DATE:

DAVID AND HIS MIGHTY MEN — DAVID'S MEN WERE MIGHTY BECAUSE GOD WAS WITH THEM

When David fled to a cave years before, 400 discontented men gathered to him (1 Samuel 22). Some would become David's mighty men. What makes you a mighty man or woman of God? It's not about your strength. It's about your faith. Spiritually-mighty people believe God's love, love God, and rely on the power of the Holy Spirit. Are you a mighty man or woman of God?

153

READING

They shall be like mighty men, Who tread down their enemies In the mire of the streets in the battle. They shall fight because the Lord is with them, And the riders on horses shall be put to shame. (Zechariah 10:5)

SCRIPTURE READINGS:

- 2 Samuel 23:8-39
- 1 Chronicles 11:10
- Zechariah 10:5

Questions? Learnings? Praises? Prayers? To Do's? Jesus is...?

DATE:

154
REFLECTION AND PRAYER

Look Back at Last Week — List what God did and what God taught you over the last week. This is your "thank God list" for next week.

Look Forward to Next Week — List what events, decisions, deadlines, or progress needs to happen in the next week. This is your prayer list for next week.

DATE:

DAVID'S FOOLISH CENSUS — DAVID'S PRIDE, GOD'S JUDGMENT, AND DAVID'S SACRIFICE

When God became angry with Israel, He let Satan tempt their leader to count the people. David counted the people out of arrogance, not care and concern. Joab asked David about his motives. What are your motives these days? Why are you doing what you're doing? God resists the arrogant (1 Peter 5:5). Is Jesus filling your heart with His love, humility, and submission?

> *Now Satan stood up against Israel, and moved David to number Israel. So David said to Joab and to the leaders of the people, "Go, number Israel from Beersheba to Dan, and bring the number of them to me that I may know it." (1 Chronicles 21:1-2)*

SCRIPTURE READINGS:

- 2 Samuel 24
- 1 Chronicles 21:1-4
- 1 Chronicles 27:23-24

Questions? Learnings? Praises? Prayers? To Do's? Jesus is...?

DATE:

156 READING

SOLOMON AND THE THRONE — ADONIJAH'S REBELLION, DAVID'S DEATH, AND A PSALM OF PRAYER FOR THE KING

David prepared Solomon to be a king who kept God's word and helped others follow God. Psalm 72 was a prayer for those things, from "Give the king your judgments" to "Let the whole earth be filled with Your glory." Jesus wants to do this through you too. Every Christian is a king (Revelation 1:6). Are you keeping Jesus' word? Are you spreading His glory around the world?

> *Now the days of David drew near that he should die, and he charged Solomon his son, saying: "...keep the charge of the Lord your God: to walk in His ways, to keep His statutes, His commandments, His judgments, and His testimonies, as it is written in the Law of Moses, that you may prosper in all that you do and wherever you turn; (1 Kings 2:1, 3)*

SCRIPTURE READINGS:

- 1 Kings 1
- 1 Kings 2
- Psalm 72

Questions? Learnings? Praises? Prayers? To Do's? Jesus is...?

DATE:

SOLOMON AND HIS PRAYER — GOD'S VISIT TO SOLOMON, SOLOMON'S PRAYER, DIVIDING THE CHILD, AND THE WORD

157 READING

If God gave you one wish, what would it be? Solomon asked God for wisdom to lead. Pause and ask God for wisdom right now. Christ is the wisdom of God (1 Corinthians 1:24). One time, Solomon didn't know which of two mothers' babies was alive. Solomon produced a sword which revealed the truth. The sword pictured the Bible which reveals truth (Hebrews 4:12-13).

Therefore give to Your servant an understanding heart to judge Your people, that I may discern between good and evil. For who is able to judge this great people of Yours?" (1 Kings 3:9)

SCRIPTURE READINGS:

- 1 Kings 3
- Matthew 7:7-11
- Hebrews 4:12-13

Questions? Learnings? Praises? Prayers? To Do's? Jesus is...?

DATE:

158 READING

SOLOMON AND HIS WISDOM — SOLOMON'S 3000 PROVERBS AND 1005 SONGS

Solomon was a prolific author who wrote 3000 proverbs (the entire book of Proverbs has 915 verses) and 1005 songs (including Psalm 72, 127, and Song of Solomon). God inspired Solomon to write, "A wise man will hear and increase learning." When you read the Bible, you're learning about Jesus' mind, His heart, and His wisdom — and God is transforming you like Him.

> *A wise man will hear and increase learning, And a man of understanding will attain wise counsel… The fear of the Lord is the beginning of knowledge, But fools despise wisdom and instruction. (Proverbs 1:5, 7)*

SCRIPTURE READINGS:

- 1 Kings 4:29-34
- Proverbs 1
- Song 1

Questions? Learnings? Praises? Prayers? To Do's? Jesus is…?

DATE:

SOLOMON AND THE TEMPLE — BUILDING SOLOMON'S TEMPLE, BUILDING A HOUSE, AND BUILDING THE CHURCH

Solomon's temple pictured Jesus' church. The temple was built with physical stones; the church is a temple built with "living stones" (people). The temple stones were placed silently; the Holy Spirit draws people to the church silently. God called the world to meet Him at Solomon's temple; God sends the church (i.e. you) to take Jesus to the world. Jesus is building His church.

> [Christians] having been built on the foundation of the apostles and prophets, Jesus Christ Himself being the chief cornerstone, in whom the whole building, being fitted together, grows into a holy temple in the Lord, (Ephesians 2:20-21)

SCRIPTURE READINGS:

- 1 Kings 6
- Psalm 127
- Ephesians 2:19-22

Questions? Learnings? Praises? Prayers? To Do's? Jesus is…?

DATE:

160 READING

SOLOMON AND THE TEMPLE — SOLOMON'S SPEECH, SOLOMON'S PRAYER, AND GOD'S SECOND VISIT TO SOLOMON

At the Temple dedication, Solomon raised his hands in prayer. "There is no God like You." After the dedication, God appeared to Solomon a second time. "Keep my statutes and I'll establish your throne forever." Sadly, Solomon failed to keep God's statutes. Where Solomon failed, Jesus succeeded. Do you believe the gospel of Jesus? Where you failed, Jesus succeeded.

So the Lord has fulfilled His word which He spoke; and I have filled the position of my father David, and sit on the throne of Israel, as the Lord promised; and I have built a temple for the name of the Lord God of Israel. (1 Kings 8:20)

SCRIPTURE READINGS:

- 1 Kings 8
- 1 Kings 9:1-9
- 1 Kings 11:9-10

Questions? Learnings? Praises? Prayers? To Do's? Jesus is...?

DATE:

161
REFLECTION AND PRAYER

Look Back at Last Week — List what God did and what God taught you over the last week. This is your "thank God list" for next week.

Look Forward to Next Week — List what events, decisions, deadlines, or progress needs to happen in the next week. This is your prayer list for next week.

DATE:

162 READING

SOLOMON AND THE QUEEN OF SHEBA — SOLOMON, JESUS, AND US BEING READY TO ANSWER QUESTIONS

As word spread about Solomon, God spread His own fame and glory. The queen of Sheba (southern Arabia) came to test Solomon with hard questions. She was stunned by hearing God's wisdom and seeing God's love. Solomon pictured how Jesus wants to spread His fame through you: by sharing His wisdom with humility and being a living expression of God's love.

> *The queen of the South will rise up in the judgment with this generation and condemn it, for she came from the ends of the earth to hear the wisdom of Solomon; and indeed a greater than Solomon [Jesus] is here. (Matthew 12:42)*

SCRIPTURE READINGS:

- 1 Kings 10:1-13
- Matthew 12:42
- 1 Peter 3:15

Questions? Learnings? Praises? Prayers? To Do's? Jesus is...?

DATE:

SOLOMON AND HIS WEALTH — SOLOMON'S WEALTH AND HIS THOUGHTS ON THE LIMITATIONS OF WEALTH

God gave Solomon unimaginable wealth and wisdom about the challenges of money. Solomon wrote that if you have more, you'll have higher expenses and greater worries about losing it. He wrote that if you love money, you'll never have enough of it to satisfy you. Do you believe both of those statements? God created you with a deep need for Jesus that money can never fill.

He who loves silver will not be satisfied with silver; Nor he who loves abundance, with increase. This also is vanity. When goods increase, They increase who eat them; So what profit have the owners Except to see them with their eyes? (Ecclesiastes 5:10–11)

SCRIPTURE READINGS:

- 1 Kings 10:14-29
- Ecclesiastes 2:1-11
- Ecclesiastes 5:10-20

Questions? Learnings? Praises? Prayers? To Do's? Jesus is…?

DATE:

164 READING

SOLOMON AND HIS WIVES — SOLOMON'S WIVES TURN SOLOMON'S HEART AWAY FROM GOD

God warned kings not to multiply horses, wives, or gold. Solomon relentlessly pursued more of all three. What are you pursuing these days? More or Jesus? Solomon's power and wealth let him marry 700 wives and 300 concubines. His spouses drew his heart away from God. Jesus designed marriage as one man and one woman helping each other love and serve God.

> And it [his Bible] shall be with him, and he shall read it all the days of his life, that he may learn to fear the Lord his God and be careful to observe all the words of this law and these statutes, that his heart may not be lifted above his brethren, that he may not turn aside from the commandment to the right hand or to the left... (Deuteronomy 17:19-20)

SCRIPTURE READINGS:

- 1 Kings 11:1-40
- Deuteronomy 17:14-20
- Nehemiah 13:25-31

Questions? Learnings? Praises? Prayers? To Do's? Jesus is...?

DATE:

SOLOMON AND HIS DEATH — SOLOMON'S FINAL COMMENTS ON THE MEANING OF LIFE

165 READING

God gave Solomon all the resources needed (wisdom, money, power, peace) to experiment with different approaches to life. He tried laughter, pleasure, learning, collecting, constructing, accomplishing, family, friendship, etc. In the end, Solomon realized that the only thing that will matter someday is how you related to God. Is your life about loving and following Jesus?

> *Let us hear the conclusion of the whole matter:*
> *Fear God and keep His commandments,*
> *For this is man's all. (Ecclesiastes 12:13)*

SCRIPTURE READINGS:

- 1 Kings 11:41-43
- Ecclesiastes 1
- Ecclesiastes 12

Questions? Learnings? Praises? Prayers? To Do's? Jesus is...?

DATE:

166 READING

REHOBOAM (SOUTHERN KING 17 YEARS) — REHOBOAM IGNORES THE WISDOM OF ANSWERING GENTLY

The northern tribes asked the new king Rehoboam to lighten Solomon's heavy burdens. Older counselors recommended Rehoboam serve his people and speak kindly. Rehoboam didn't. Jesus' leadership was revolutionary. He led people by becoming their servant. He called His disciples to do the same. Is Jesus influencing people through you with kindness and service?

A soft answer turns away wrath, But a harsh word stirs up anger. (Proverbs 15:1)

SCRIPTURE READINGS:

- 1 Kings 12:1-24
- 1 Kings 14:21-30
- Proverbs 15:1

Questions? Learnings? Praises? Prayers? To Do's? Jesus is…?

DATE:

JEROBOAM (NORTHERN KING 22 YEARS) — JEROBOAM CREATES IDOLS TO KEEP THE PEOPLE'S ALLEGIANCE

God told Jeroboam that, because Solomon left God, He would divide Israel and have Jeroboam lead the 10 northern tribes (1 Kings 11). Jeroboam heard God but he didn't trust God. He feared losing people to the southern tribes so he invented a false religion. Are you fully trusting Jesus these days? Or, out of fear, are you trying to control people and circumstances yourself?

167
READING

> *Therefore the king asked advice, made two calves of gold, and said to the people, "It is too much for you to go up to Jerusalem. Here are your gods, O Israel, which brought you up from the land of Egypt!" (1 Kings 12:28)*

SCRIPTURE READINGS:

- 1 Kings 12:25-33
- 1 Kings 13
- 1 Kings 14:1-20

Questions? Learnings? Praises? Prayers? To Do's? Jesus is...?

DATE:

168
REFLECTION AND PRAYER

Look Back at Last Week — List what God did and what God taught you over the last week. This is your "thank God list" for next week.

Look Forward to Next Week — List what events, decisions, deadlines, or progress needs to happen in the next week. This is your prayer list for next week.

DATE:

ASA (SOUTHERN KING 41 YEARS) — ASA RELIES ON SYRIA INSTEAD OF RELYING ON THE LORD

169 READING

King Asa followed God all 41 years of his reign but didn't always trust God. When attacked, he trusted the king of Syria to protect him. His plan worked but God was not pleased. When Jesus walked the earth, He followed God and trusted Him. Are you following and trusting God in the power of the Holy Spirit? Or are you trusting your plans, partners, or money to protect you?

> *...Because you have relied on the king of Syria, and have not relied on the Lord your God, therefore the army of the king of Syria has escaped from your hand... For the eyes of the Lord run to and fro throughout the whole earth, to show Himself strong on behalf of those whose heart is loyal to Him... (2 Chronicles 16:7, 9)*

SCRIPTURE READINGS:

- 1 Kings 15:1-24
- 2 Chronicles 16:1-14
- Psalms 118:5-14

Questions? Learnings? Praises? Prayers? To Do's? Jesus is...?

DATE:

170 READING

FIVE WICKED KINGS (NORTHERN KINGS 40 YEARS) — THE SINS OF FIVE DIFFERENT KINGS AND GOD'S ANGER

King Jeroboam left a spiritual legacy of generations of kings rebelling against God like him: Jeroboam's son Nadab; Nadab's murderer Baasha; Baasha's son Elah; Elah's murderer Zimri; Zimri's replacement Omri. Jesus created you to leave a spiritual legacy too: of godliness, loving Jesus, loving people, and following Him. What is the spiritual legacy you are leaving?

> *Inasmuch as I lifted you [Baasha] out of the dust and made you ruler over My people Israel, and you have walked in the way of Jeroboam, and have made My people Israel sin, to provoke Me to anger with their sins, (1 Kings 16:2)*

SCRIPTURE READINGS:

- 1 Kings 15:25-33
- 1 Kings 16:1-28
- Isaiah 65:2-3

Questions? Learnings? Praises? Prayers? To Do's? Jesus is…?

DATE:

AHAB (NORTHERN KING 22 YEARS) — ELIJAH'S POWERFUL PRAYER AND DROUGHT OF THREE AND A HALF YEARS

King Ahab continued Jeroboam's evil legacy but was worse. God sent Elijah to call Ahab to turn to God. When Elijah prayed, it didn't rain for three and a half years. When he prayed again, it rained. Elijah showed that one person who prays God's will can make a huge difference. Your prayers matter. Pray now for Jesus to be known and God's will to be done around the world.

Confess your trespasses to one another, and pray for one another, that you may be healed. The effective, fervent prayer of a righteous man avails much. Elijah was a man with a nature like ours, and he prayed earnestly that it would not rain; and it did not rain on the land for three years and six months. (James 5:16–17)

SCRIPTURE READINGS:

- 1 Kings 16:29-34
- 1 Kings 17
- James 5:16-18

Questions? Learnings? Praises? Prayers? To Do's? Jesus is…?

DATE:

172 READING

AHAB (NORTHERN KING 22 YEARS) — ELIJAH'S VICTORY, THE FIRES FROM HEAVEN, AND END OF THE DROUGHT

At Mount Carmel, the LORD showed that He is the one true God. When the false prophets prayed, nothing happened. When Elijah prayed, God answered with fire. One time, James and John asked Jesus to call down fire from heaven like Elijah did. Jesus told them he came to save people not destroy them. Is Jesus moving you to want God to save people instead of destroy?

> *But He [Jesus] turned and rebuked them, and said, "You do not know what manner of spirit you are of. For the Son of Man did not come to destroy men's lives but to save them." And they went to another village. (Luke 9:55-56)*

SCRIPTURE READINGS:

- 1 Kings 18
- 2 Kings 1:1-15
- Luke 9:51-56

Questions? Learnings? Praises? Prayers? To Do's? Jesus is…?

DATE:

AHAB (NORTHERN KING 22 YEARS) — ELIJAH'S DEPRESSION, GOD'S COMPASSION, THE 7000, AND ELISHA

After Mount Carmel, Jezebel threatened to kill Elijah. He fled depressed and alone. The Bible talks openly about depression: when your soul is cast down or brought low. Jesus experienced being down and alone too. He sympathizes with you (Hebrews 4:15-16). You are not alone. Jesus can use the seasons of depression in your life to give you new direction as He did Elijah.

173 READING

> *As a father pities his children, So the LORD pities those who fear Him. For He knows our frame; He remembers that we are dust. (Psalm 103:13–14)*

SCRIPTURE READINGS:

- 1 Kings 19
- Psalms 103:13-14
- Romans 11:1-8

Questions? Learnings? Praises? Prayers? To Do's? Jesus is…?

DATE:

174 READING

AHAB (NORTHERN KING 22 YEARS) — SYRIA'S THREATS AND NABOTH'S VINEYARD

God graciously kept revealing Himself to evil King Ahab. After defeating the Syrians, God said, "You shall know that I am the LORD." After Ahab spared Syria's king and murdered Naboth, God said He'd judge him. When Ahab humbled himself, God showed mercy. That's Jesus. He reveals Himself and is always merciful to the humble. Are you humbling yourself before Jesus?

> "See how Ahab has humbled himself before Me? Because he has humbled himself before Me, I will not bring the calamity in his days. In the days of his son I will bring the calamity on his house." (1 Kings 21:29)

SCRIPTURE READINGS:

- 1 Kings 20
- 1 Kings 21
- 2 Kings 9:24-26

Questions? Learnings? Praises? Prayers? To Do's? Jesus is...?

DATE:

175

REFLECTION AND PRAYER

Look Back at Last Week — List what God did and what God taught you over the last week. This is your "thank God list" for next week.

Look Forward to Next Week — List what events, decisions, deadlines, or progress needs to happen in the next week. This is your prayer list for next week.

DATE:

176 READING

AHAB (NORTHERN KING 22 YEARS) — MICAIAH'S PROPHECY, SAYING WHAT GOD SAYS, AND AHAB'S DEATH

Ahab hated the prophet Micaiah. He wanted Michaiah to say nice things. Michaiah said God's things. Would you rather people say you're nice or God say you're faithful? How is it nice to hide God's truth from someone? You can share Jesus with kindness. Are you letting Jesus, the Faithful and True Witness, lead you to be a kind and faithful witness for Him (Revelation 3:14)?

And Micaiah said, "As the Lord lives, whatever the Lord says to me, that I will speak." (1 Kings 22:14)

SCRIPTURE READINGS:

- 2 Chronicles 18:1-4
- 1 Kings 22:1-40
- Jeremiah 42:1-6

Questions? Learnings? Praises? Prayers? To Do's? Jesus is...?

DATE:

JEHOSHAPHAT (SOUTHERN KING 25 YEARS) — JEHOSHAPHAT'S REFORMS AND SINGERS ON THE BATTLEFRONT

Jehosaphat was a good king with bad friends. He took away idols but helped Israel's evil kings. Before one battle, God told Jehosphat that he would win without needing to fight. Jehosphat believed God so much that they sent musicians out to praise God before the army. Like Jehoshaphat, do you trust Jesus so much that you praise Him before you see Him move?

177 READING

And Jehu… said to King Jehoshaphat, "Should you help the wicked and love those who hate the Lord? Therefore the wrath of the Lord is upon you. Nevertheless good things are found in you, in that you have removed the wooden images from the land, and have prepared your heart to seek God." (2 Chronicles 19:2-3)

SCRIPTURE READINGS:

- 2 Chronicles 19
- 2 Chronicles 20
- 1 Kings 22:41-50

Questions? Learnings? Praises? Prayers? To Do's? Jesus is…?

DATE:

TIM HOWEY

178 READING

JEHORAM (SOUTHERN KING 8 YEARS) — GOD'S PROMISE TO DAVID AND ELIJAH'S LETTER TO JEHORAM

When Jehoram became king, he did evil after evil. Other evil kings had their line wiped out but, a century and a half before, God promised David that his descendant (Jesus) would reign on the throne. No one can stop God's promises. If you have Jesus, He's promised to forgive your sins, live inside you, and give you eternal life. No one (not even you) can stop His promises to you.

The Lord has sworn in truth to David; He will not turn from it: "I will set upon your throne the fruit of your body. (Psalm 132:11)

SCRIPTURE READINGS:

- 2 Chronicles 21
- 2 Samuel 7:16-17
- Psalms 132:10-12

Questions? Learnings? Praises? Prayers? To Do's? Jesus is...?

DATE:

ELISHA AND ELIJAH — THE CHARIOT OF FIRE, PASSING THE MANTLE, THE SPRINGS OF JERICHO, AND ELIJAH'S RETURN

Elijah and Elisha were prophets who pictured Jesus. Elijah ascended to heaven as people watched and will return like Jesus. Elisha gave a man sight and healed a leper like Jesus. Both raised the dead like Jesus. Their miracles also picture what Jesus does for you if you have Him. Jesus healed you and helped you see spiritually. One day, He will raise you from the dead too.

179 READING

And so it was, when they had crossed over, that Elijah said to Elisha, "Ask! What may I do for you, before I am taken away from you?" Elisha said, "Please let a double portion of your spirit be upon me." (2 Kings 2:9)

SCRIPTURE READINGS:

- 2 Kings 2
- John 1:19-28
- Matthew 17:1-13

Questions? Learnings? Praises? Prayers? To Do's? Jesus is…?

DATE:

180 READING

ELISHA AND THE DITCHES — DIGGING DITCHES FOR WAR AND THE MIRACLE OF THE BREAD

Elisha pictured Jesus. He protected Israel, cared for widows, raised a dead son, and multiplied bread like Jesus. Elisha fed 100 prophets with 20 loaves. Jesus fed 5,000 men (plus others) with five loaves. Jesus said this miracle pictured Him, the bread of life. He fills your soul and miraculously provides for others when you share Him. Are you sharing Jesus, the bread of life?

> *Therefore they gathered them up, and filled twelve baskets with the fragments of the five barley loaves which were left over by those who had eaten. Then those men, when they had seen the sign that Jesus did, said, "This is truly the Prophet who is to come into the world." (John 6:13-14)*

SCRIPTURE READINGS:

- 2 Kings 3
- 2 Kings 4
- John 6:1-14

Questions? Learnings? Praises? Prayers? To Do's? Jesus is...?

DATE:

ELISHA AND NAAMAN — ELISHA HEALS NAAMAN THE LEPER AND JESUS HEALS LEPERS

Namaan was a leper. Leprosy pictures sin: contagious; crippling; killing your ability to feel. Namaan's healing pictured salvation: simple; counter-intuitive; exercising faith in God's word. Jesus touched lepers but didn't contract leprosy; He healed it. He wants to heal your sin too. Jesus said Namaan shows God's grace to non-Jewish people. God's grace is for you too.

181 READING

Then He [Jesus] put out His hand and touched him, saying, "I am willing; be cleansed." Immediately the leprosy left him. (Luke 5:13)

SCRIPTURE READINGS:

- 2 Kings 5
- Luke 4:16-30
- Luke 5:12-15

Questions? Learnings? Praises? Prayers? To Do's? Jesus is…?

DATE:

182
REFLECTION AND PRAYER

Look Back at Last Week — List what God did and what God taught you over the last week. This is your "thank God list" for next week.

Look Forward to Next Week — List what events, decisions, deadlines, or progress needs to happen in the next week. This is your prayer list for next week.

DATE:

ELISHA AND HIS PRAYER — SEEING THE INVISIBLE SPIRITUAL REALM ALL AROUND US

One night, the Syrians surrounded Elisha and his servant. When the servant woke, he thought they were surrounded. Elisha knew God had the Syrians surrounded. Elisha asked God to open his servant's eyes spiritually. Jesus is surrounding and protecting you too even when you can't see Him. Are you looking at the world physically or spiritually? Jesus has your problems surrounded.

183
READING

> *So he answered, "Do not fear, for those who are with us are more than those who are with them." And Elisha prayed, and said, "Lord, I pray, open his eyes that he may see." Then the Lord opened the eyes of the young man, and he saw. And behold, the mountain was full of horses and chariots of fire all around Elisha. (2 Kings 6:16–17)*

SCRIPTURE READINGS:

- 2 Kings 6:1-23
- 2 Kings 2:11
- 2 Chronicles 32:6-8

Questions? Learnings? Praises? Prayers? To Do's? Jesus is...?

DATE:

184 READING

ELISHA AND THE FAMINE — THE FOUR LEPERS' DECISION IN A FAMINE AND ELISHA'S DEATH

The capital of Samaria was besieged and starving. This pictured the spiritual starvation of not hearing God's words (Amos 8:11). The Syrians fled. Food and riches were waiting in the Syrians' tents but people didn't know. Today, spiritual food and riches are waiting in Jesus but people don't know. Are you being filled with Christ's riches and sharing the news with others?

> *For the Lord had caused the army of the Syrians to hear the noise of chariots and the noise of horses—the noise of a great army; so they said to one another, "Look, the king of Israel has hired against us the kings of the Hittites and the kings of the Egyptians to attack us!" (2 Kings 7:6)*

SCRIPTURE READINGS:

- 2 Kings 6:24-33
- 2 Kings 7
- Kings 13:14-21

Questions? Learnings? Praises? Prayers? To Do's? Jesus is...?

DATE:

JEHU (NORTHERN KING 28 YEARS) — JEHU KILLS AHAB'S FAMILY ACCORDING TO ELIJAH'S PROPHECY

God said Ahab's royal line would be wiped out for his sins (1 Kings 21:21). God anointed Jehu as king of Israel to do it. Jehu went beyond what God said and executed Ahab's friends and the southern kingdom's royal line. Out of zeal, Jehu took vengeance in his own hands. Jesus wants you to be passionate for justice. But are you so passionate that you take vengeance yourself?

> But Jehu took no heed to walk in the law of the Lord God of Israel with all his heart; for he did not depart from the sins of Jeroboam, who had made Israel sin. (2 Kings 10:31)

SCRIPTURE READINGS:

- 2 Kings 9
- 2 Kings 10
- Hosea 1:2-5

Questions? Learnings? Praises? Prayers? To Do's? Jesus is...?

DATE:

186 READING

ATHALIAH (SOUTHERN QUEEN 6 YEARS) AND JOASH (SOUTHERN KING 41 YEARS) — LEADERS AND FOLLOWING GOD

When Athaliah's son died, she killed the royal heirs and made herself queen. Baby Joash survived. Seven years later, Jehoiada the high priest anointed Joash as king. While Jehoiadah lived, Joash followed God. When his spiritual mentor died, Joash stopped following God. Who are your spiritual mentors helping you follow Jesus? Who are you helping to follow Jesus?

Joash did what was right in the sight of the Lord all the days of Jehoiada the priest. (2 Chronicles 24:2)

SCRIPTURE READINGS:

- 2 Kings 11
- 2 Chronicles 24
- Deuteronomy 28:25-26

Questions? Learnings? Praises? Prayers? To Do's? Jesus is…?

DATE:

AMAZIAH (SOUTHERN KING 29 YEARS) — LOSING MONEY AND THE RIGHT ATTITUDE TOWARD WEALTH

Out of fear, King Amaziah hired 100,000 mercenaries for 100 talents of silver. Amaziah trusted his money and connections instead of God. God told Amaziah to send them home. Amaziah asked about the money he invested. God said let it go. He could give Amaziah more money. Your money isn't yours. It's Jesus' money. Are you managing Jesus' money like He wants?

187
READING

And you shall remember the Lord your God, for it is He who gives you power to get wealth, that He may establish His covenant which He swore to your fathers, as it is this day. (Deuteronomy 8:18)

SCRIPTURE READINGS:

- 2 Kings 14:1-4
- 2 Chronicles 25
- Deuteronomy 8:18

Questions? Learnings? Praises? Prayers? To Do's? Jesus is…?

DATE:

188 READING

JONAH FLEES AND PRAYS — GOD CALLS JONAH DURING THE REIGN OF JEROBOAM II (NORTHERN KING 41 YEARS)

When God sent Jonah to the wicked king of Israel, he went. When God sent Jonah to the wicked people of Nineveh, he fled. Jonah tried to run from God and God's call. Are you running from God? After Jonah was swallowed, he pictured Jesus: weeds wrapped around his head (crown of thorns); for three days and nights (burial); then he appeared again (resurrection).

> "Arise, go to Nineveh, that great city, and cry out against it; for their wickedness has come up before Me." But Jonah arose to flee to Tarshish from the presence of the Lord. He went down to Joppa, and found a ship going to Tarshish; so he paid the fare, and went down into it, to go with them to Tarshish from the presence of the Lord. (Jonah 1:2–3)

SCRIPTURE READINGS:

- 2 Kings 14:23-29
- Jonah 1
- Jonah 2

Questions? Learnings? Praises? Prayers? To Do's? Jesus is…?

DATE:

189
REFLECTION AND PRAYER

Look Back at Last Week — List what God did and what God taught you over the last week. This is your "thank God list" for next week.

Look Forward to Next Week — List what events, decisions, deadlines, or progress needs to happen in the next week. This is your prayer list for next week.

DATE:

190 READING

JONAH PREACHES AND POUTS — JONAH'S HARDNESS TOWARD THE ASSYRIANS OF NINEVEH AND GOD'S MERCY

After Jonah was vomited on the shore, God told him again to go to Nineveh. This time he obeyed. In your life, Jesus is willing to use difficult times to help you to follow Him too. Jonah preached but hoped no one listened. Jonah cared about his comfort and a plant, not people. If Jesus is in you, you will start to care for people far from God in foreign nations. Is Jesus in you?

> *For as Jonah was three days and three nights in the belly of the great fish, so will the Son of Man [Jesus] be three days and three nights in the heart of the earth. The men of Nineveh will rise up in the judgment with this generation and condemn it, because they repented at the preaching of Jonah; and indeed a greater than Jonah [Jesus] is here. (Matthew 12:40-41)*

SCRIPTURE READINGS:

- Jonah 3
- Jonah 4
- Matthew 12:38-41

Questions? Learnings? Praises? Prayers? To Do's? Jesus is...?

DATE:

UZZIAH'S LIFE (SOUTHERN KING 52 YEARS) — UZZIAH GROWS ARROGANT WHEN HE IS STRONG AND LEPROSY

King Uzziah started well. As long as he sought the LORD, God made him prosper. When you seek Jesus, He will bless you too. Are you seeking Jesus? When Uzziah became successful, he grew arrogant and took the priest's role. He contracted leprosy and God stopped helping him. God resists the proud but gives grace to the humble. Are you humbling yourself before Jesus?

191
READING

But when he was strong his heart was lifted up, to his destruction, for he transgressed against the Lord his God by entering the temple of the Lord to burn incense on the altar of incense. (2 Chronicles 26:16)

SCRIPTURE READINGS:

- 2 Chronicles 26
- Proverbs 29:22-23
- Leviticus 13:45-46

Questions? Learnings? Praises? Prayers? To Do's? Jesus is…?

DATE:

192 READING

UZZIAH'S DEATH (SOUTHERN KING 52 YEARS) — UZZIAH DIES, GOD CALLS ISAIAH, AND SEEING HEAVEN

Isaiah watched Uzziah grow arrogant and die alone. Then God showed him a vision of Himself in heaven. Shocked by God's holiness, Isaiah confessed his and Israel's sins. God purged his sins and asked, "Who will go for Us [Father, Son, and Spirit]?" Isaiah said, "Send me." Do you know how great and holy Jesus is? If you do, you'll confess your sins and do whatever He says.

Also I heard the voice of the Lord, saying: "Whom shall I send, And who will go for Us?" Then I said, "Here am I! Send me." (Isaiah 6:8)

SCRIPTURE READINGS:

- 2 Chronicles 26:22-23
- Isaiah 6
- Revelation 4

Questions? Learnings? Praises? Prayers? To Do's? Jesus is…?

DATE:

HOSHEA (NORTHERN KING 9 YEARS) — THE NORTHERN KINGDOM'S CAPTIVITY AND HISTORY OF THE SAMARITANS

The northern tribes worshiped idols for two centuries. Finally, God let the Assyrians take them into captivity and move Gentiles to their land. The Jews and Gentiles who married and created a new religion were called Samaritans. The Jews hated Samaritans. Jesus loved Samaritans and challenged Jewish racism. Do you sense Jesus in you challenging racism and loving all people?

Then the woman of Samaria said to Him [Jesus], "How is it that You, being a Jew, ask a drink from me, a Samaritan woman?" For Jews have no dealings with Samaritans. (John 4:9)

SCRIPTURE READINGS:

- 2 Kings 17
- John 8:45-49
- John 4:1-9

Questions? Learnings? Praises? Prayers? To Do's? Jesus is…?

DATE:

194 READING

HEZEKIAH (SOUTHERN KING 29 YEARS) — KING HEZEKIAH'S SPIRITUAL REFORMS AND HIS PASSOVER

No king trusted God like Hezekiah. He cleansed the temple, destroyed every false idol, and led people to worship God again. Jesus wants to do that in you spiritually: cleanse the temple of your body (1 Corinthians 6); remove every false priority that's taking your affection from Him; lead you to worship Him again. Will you trust Jesus like Hezekiah and make Him your first love?

> *For if you return to the Lord, your brethren and your children will be treated with compassion by those who lead them captive, so that they may come back to this land; for the Lord your God is gracious and merciful, and will not turn His face from you if you return to Him."* (2 Chronicles 30:9)

SCRIPTURE READINGS:

- 2 Kings 18:1-8
- 2 Chronicles 29
- 2 Chronicles 30

Questions? Learnings? Praises? Prayers? To Do's? Jesus is…?

DATE:

HEZEKIAH (SOUTHERN KING 29 YEARS) — HEZEKIAH FIGHTS THE ASSYRIANS AND COPIES THE PROVERBS

When the Assyrians attacked the southern tribes after defeating the north, Isaiah prayed. God said, "Don't fear their words." Hezekiah received a threatening letter and prayed, "Save us so people know You are God." God defended Jerusalem for His name's sake. Do you, like Isaiah, pray when you face trials? Do you, like Hezekiah, ask Jesus to move so His fame grows?

And Hezekiah received the letter from the hand of the messengers, and read it; and Hezekiah went up to the house of the Lord, and spread it before the Lord... "Now therefore, O Lord our God, I pray, save us from his hand, that all the kingdoms of the earth may know that You are the Lord God, You alone." (2 Kings 19:14, 19)

SCRIPTURE READINGS:

- 2 Kings 18:9-37
- 2 Kings 19
- Proverbs 25:1-7

Questions? Learnings? Praises? Prayers? To Do's? Jesus is…?

DATE:

196
REFLECTION AND PRAYER

Look Back at Last Week — List what God did and what God taught you over the last week. This is your "thank God list" for next week.

Look Forward to Next Week — List what events, decisions, deadlines, or progress needs to happen in the next week. This is your prayer list for next week.

DATE:

HEZEKIAH (SOUTHERN KING 29 YEARS) — GOD EXTENDS HEZEKIAH'S LIFE, ISAIAH'S REGRET, AND BABYLON

King Hezekiah was dying in his thirties when he begged God for more time. God gave him 15 more years. In those 15 years, he grew arrogant, showed his treasures to the Babylonians, and raised evil King Manasseh. Isaiah saw this and noted that, sometimes, good people die young to protect them from something worse. Do you realize that death might be Jesus' protection?

The righteous perishes, And no man takes it to heart; Merciful men are taken away, While no one considers That the righteous is taken away from evil. (Isaiah 57:1)

SCRIPTURE READINGS:

- 2 Kings 20
- Isaiah 57:1
- 2 Chronicles 32:24-33

Questions? Learnings? Praises? Prayers? To Do's? Jesus is...?

DATE:

198 READING

MANASSEH (SOUTHERN KING 55 YEARS) — MANASSEH'S SIN, JUDGMENT, AND REPENTANCE

King Manasseh undid all his dad's reforms. He rebuilt the idols, consulted psychics, murdered people, and ignored God's messengers. His kingdom became more evil than nations who didn't know God. Have you ever thought God couldn't reach someone? When the Assyrians enslaved Manasseh, his heart turned back to God. Manasseh's story is hope that God can reach anyone.

> *"But if a wicked man turns from all his sins which he has committed, keeps all My statutes, and does what is lawful and right, he shall surely live; he shall not die... Do I have any pleasure at all that the wicked should die?" says the Lord God, "and not that he should turn from his ways and live? (Ezekiel 18:21, 23)*

SCRIPTURE READINGS:

- 2 Kings 21:1-16
- 2 Chronicles 33
- Ezekiel 18:21-32

Questions? Learnings? Praises? Prayers? To Do's? Jesus is...?

DATE:

JOSIAH (SOUTHERN KING 31 YEARS) — GOD CALLS JOSIAH AND JEREMIAH TO INFLUENCE A SINFUL NATION

Josiah was Judah's last good king. He became king at eight, sought God at 16, and destroyed all their idols at 20. Then God called Jeremiah (likely in his late teens) to preach. Jeremiah said, "I can't speak. I'm a youth." God said he wasn't too young. Jesus calls young people to salvation and service today. Do you watch for it? Encourage it? Prioritize ministry to kids and students?

> *Then said I: "Ah, Lord God! Behold, I cannot speak, for I am a youth." But the Lord said to me: "Do not say, 'I am a youth,' For you shall go to all to whom I send you, And whatever I command you, you shall speak. (Jeremiah 1:6–7)*

SCRIPTURE READINGS:

- 2 Chronicles 34:1-7
- Jeremiah 1
- Jeremiah 25:3-9

Questions? Learnings? Praises? Prayers? To Do's? Jesus is…?

DATE:

READING

JOSIAH (SOUTHERN KING 31 YEARS) — JOSIAH DISCOVERS THE BIBLE AND HUMBLES HIMSELF BEFORE GOD

No king turned to God like Josiah. When the priests discovered their copy of the Bible in the temple, they read it to Josiah. God spoke to Josiah through words written centuries before. Josiah said, "Great is the wrath on us [today]." Jesus wants you to read the Bible like Josiah. When you read God's words from centuries before, do you listen for God to speak to you today?

> *because your [Josiah's] heart was tender, and you humbled yourself before God when you heard His words against this place and against its inhabitants, and you humbled yourself before Me, and you tore your clothes and wept before Me, I also have heard you," says the Lord. (2 Chronicles 34:27)*

SCRIPTURE READINGS:

- 2 Chronicles 34:8-28
- 2 Kings 23:1-27
- Zephaniah 1:1-6

Questions? Learnings? Praises? Prayers? To Do's? Jesus is...?

DATE:

JOSIAH (SOUTHERN KING 31 YEARS) — JOSIAH'S PASSOVER, DYING IN THE WRONG BATTLE, AND JEHOAHAZ

When Josiah was 26, he read the Bible to Israel, committed himself and Israel to keeping God's commandments, and led a nationwide Passover. When Josiah was 39, he fought the Egyptians. God didn't call him to that fight. He was killed in a fight that wasn't his fight. Are you fighting any battles that Jesus doesn't want you to fight? Ask Jesus in prayer and listen to the Holy Spirit.

201 READING

> *He who passes by and meddles in a quarrel not his own Is like one who takes a dog by the ears. (Proverbs 26:17)*

SCRIPTURE READINGS:

- 2 Chronicles 35
- Proverbs 26:17
- 2 Chronicles 36:1-4

Questions? Learnings? Praises? Prayers? To Do's? Jesus is...?

DATE:

202 READING

JEHOIAKIM (SOUTHERN KING 11 YEARS) — JEREMIAH'S MESSAGE TO JEHOIAKIM VS. HANANIAH'S MESSAGE

King Jehoiakim replaced his brother Jehoahaz after just three months. God sent Jeremiah to the king to say Israel had to turn to God or be destroyed. Then God warned Jeremiah, "Do not diminish a word." Are you ever tempted to change God's message because it might be unpopular? You can share Jesus' message with love and grace without diminishing a word.

Thus says the Lord: "Stand in the court of the Lord's house, and speak to all the cities of Judah, which come to worship in the Lord's house, all the words that I command you to speak to them. Do not diminish a word." (Jeremiah 26:2)

SCRIPTURE READINGS:

- 2 Kings 23:31-37
- Jeremiah 26
- Jeremiah 28

Questions? Learnings? Praises? Prayers? To Do's? Jesus is...?

DATE:

203
REFLECTION AND PRAYER

Look Back at Last Week — List what God did and what God taught you over the last week. This is your "thank God list" for next week.

Look Forward to Next Week — List what events, decisions, deadlines, or progress needs to happen in the next week. This is your prayer list for next week.

DATE:

204 READING

JEHOIAKIM (SOUTHERN KING 11 YEARS) — JEREMIAH'S PROPHECY (RE: 70 YEARS) TO JEHOIAKIM DESTROYED

Jeremiah called people to worship God instead of worshiping their works. Are you living for Jesus or your activities these days? The leaders burned Jeremiah's prophecy of 70 years of captivity. Many have tried to destroy the Bible but Jesus has preserved His word. In the end, God let King Jehoiakim be taken to Babylon with the first group of exiles (2 Chronicles 36).

> *"Take a scroll of a book and write on it all the words that I have spoken to you against Israel, against Judah, and against all the nations... It may be that the house of Judah will hear all the adversities which I purpose to bring upon them, that everyone may turn from his evil way, that I may forgive their iniquity and their sin." (Jeremiah 36:2-3)*

SCRIPTURE READINGS:

- 2 Kings 24:1-7
- Jeremiah 25:1-14
- Jeremiah 36

Questions? Learnings? Praises? Prayers? To Do's? Jesus is...?

DATE:

JEHOIACHIN (SOUTHERN KING 3 MONTHS) AND ZEDEKIAH (SOUTHERN KING 11 YEARS) — JEREMIAH JAILED

King Jehoiachin reigned just three months before he was taken with 10,000 Jews to Babylon. Did you know God can use wicked leaders like Nebuchadnezzar to discipline His people? King Zedekiah heard it was God's will to serve Babylon but he rebelled against God. Jesus never rebelled against God. He always surrendered. Are you letting Jesus lead you to surrender?

Also he [Nebuchadnezzar] carried into captivity all Jerusalem: all the captains and all the mighty men of valor, ten thousand captives, and all the craftsmen and smiths. None remained except the poorest people of the land... For because of the anger of the Lord this happened... He finally cast them out from His presence... (2 Kings 24:14, 20)

SCRIPTURE READINGS:

- 2 Kings 24:8-20
- Jeremiah 37
- Jeremiah 38

Questions? Learnings? Praises? Prayers? To Do's? Jesus is...?

DATE:

206 READING

ZEDEKIAH (SOUTHERN KING 11 YEARS) — JEREMIAH LAMENTS THE FALL AND DESTRUCTION OF JERUSALEM

When King Zedekiah kept disobeying God, Nebuchadnezzar destroyed Jerusalem and took him to Babylon with the third group of Jewish exiles. Since Jeremiah trusted God through it all, God set him free. Does Jesus see you trusting Him through all your trials? When Jeremiah wrote Lamentations, he pictured Jesus mourning the blindness and destruction of Jerusalem too.

> *For I will surely deliver you [Ebed-Melech the Ethiopian], and you shall not fall by the sword; but your life shall be as a prize to you, because you have put your trust in Me," says the Lord.' " (Jeremiah 39:18)*

SCRIPTURE READINGS:

- 2 Kings 25:1-21
- Jeremiah 39
- Lamentations 2:5-19

Questions? Learnings? Praises? Prayers? To Do's? Jesus is...?

DATE:

GEDELIAH (SOUTHERN GOVERNOR 7 MONTHS) — JEREMIAH PREACHES "DON'T GO TO EGYPT" BUT IS TAKEN

The governor Gedeliah led a remnant of Jews left behind among the ruins. He urged people to serve Babylon and was murdered. People wanted to flee to Egypt but asked Jeremiah what to do. They promised, "We will obey the voice of the LORD." When God said to stay, they ignored God and fled anyway. Do you love Jesus enough to ask Him what to do, listen, and do it?

207 READING

For you were hypocrites in your hearts when you sent me to the Lord your God, saying, 'Pray for us to the Lord our God, and according to all that the Lord your God says, so declare to us and we will do it.' And I have this day declared it to you, but you have not obeyed the voice of the Lord your God, or anything which He has sent you by me. (Jeremiah 42:20-21)

SCRIPTURE READINGS:

- 2 Kings 25:22-26
- Jeremiah 42
- Jeremiah 43

Questions? Learnings? Praises? Prayers? To Do's? Jesus is…?

DATE:

DANIEL AND HIS FRIENDS OBEY GOD — DANIEL DEALS WITH TEMPTATION

Daniel, Hananiah, Mishael, and Azariah were with the first group of Jews taken to exile. The Babylonians chose them to learn their culture and serve the king. Daniel decided that he would not sin against God. Daniel pictured Jesus who was tempted to sin but didn't (Hebrews 4:15). Daniel pictured you too. Are you being tempted to sin? Jesus always creates an escape for you.

No temptation has overtaken you except such as is common to man; but God is faithful, who will not allow you to be tempted beyond what you are able, but with the temptation will also make the way of escape, that you may be able to bear it. (1 Corinthians 10:13)

SCRIPTURE READINGS:

- Daniel 1
- Proverbs 23:1-8
- 1 Corinthians 10:13

Questions? Learnings? Praises? Prayers? To Do's? Jesus is...?

DATE:

DANIEL AND NEBUCHADNEZZAR'S DREAM — DANIEL'S WISDOM AND HEARING FROM GOD

Nebuchadnezzar threatened to kill all the wise men unless they told him his dream and the interpretation. Daniel and his friends prayed. God said the dream was about future kingdoms. Then Nebuchadnezzar realized their God was the true God. When do people around you realize Jesus is the true God? When Jesus lets you face impossible situations, then delivers you.

209 READING

The king answered Daniel, and said, "Truly your God is the God of gods, the Lord of kings, and a revealer of secrets, since you could reveal this secret." (Daniel 2:47)

SCRIPTURE READINGS:

- Daniel 2
- Amos 3:7
- Ezekiel 28:1-10

Questions? Learnings? Praises? Prayers? To Do's? Jesus is...?

DATE:

210
REFLECTION AND PRAYER

Look Back at Last Week — List what God did and what God taught you over the last week. This is your "thank God list" for next week.

Look Forward to Next Week — List what events, decisions, deadlines, or progress needs to happen in the next week. This is your prayer list for next week.

DATE:

DANIEL'S THREE FRIENDS AND THE FIERY FURNACE — THE FIERY FURNACE AND FIERY TRIALS IN OUR LIVES

Shadrach, Meschach, and Abed-Nego were told to worship the king or be burned alive. They said, "God can deliver us. If He doesn't, we still won't bow." The fiery furnace pictured how Jesus is with you in your trials. He wants to protect you (from even the smell of smoke), show you He's there (the fourth man), and set you free from what is holding you back (their bindings).

211 READING

> *If that is the case, our God whom we serve is able to deliver us from the burning fiery furnace, and He will deliver us from your hand, O king. But if not, let it be known to you, O king, that we do not serve your gods, nor will we worship the gold image which you have set up." (Daniel 3:17–18)*

SCRIPTURE READINGS:

- Daniel 3
- Isaiah 48:10-11
- 1 Peter 4:12-14

Questions? Learnings? Praises? Prayers? To Do's? Jesus is...?

DATE:

212 READING

DANIEL AND NEBUCHADNEZZAR'S DREAM AND HUMBLING — GOD ESTABLISHES AUTHORITIES

Nebuchadnezzar dreamed about himself as a great tree that was cut down until knowing God gives kingdoms to whomever He chooses. One day, he arrogantly thought success was "by my mighty power." Then his dream came true and God humbled him. Do you realize your abilities and successes are a gift from God? Are you humbling yourself before Jesus and praising Him?

> *But when his [Nebuchadnezzar's] heart was lifted up, and his spirit was hardened in pride, he was deposed from his kingly throne… he was driven from the sons of men… his dwelling was with the wild donkeys… till he knew that the Most High God rules in the kingdom of men, and appoints over it whomever He chooses. (Daniel 5:20–21)*

SCRIPTURE READINGS:

- Daniel 4
- Daniel 5:18-21
- Romans 13:1-4

Questions? Learnings? Praises? Prayers? To Do's? Jesus is…?

DATE:

DANIEL AND BELSHAZZAR'S PRIDE — THE HANDWRITING OF GOD, PRIDE, AND HUMBLING YOURSELF

King Belshazzar threw a party where he praised his false gods and drank from cups stolen from the Jewish temple. Fingers wrote on the wall, "Your kingdom is over." That night, Belshazzar died. Why does God resist the proud but give grace to the humble? Because God the Son is humble. Life isn't about you. It's about Jesus. Do you continually humble yourself before God?

Likewise you younger people, submit yourselves to your elders. Yes, all of you be submissive to one another, and be clothed with humility, for "God resists the proud, But gives grace to the humble." (1 Peter 5:5)

SCRIPTURE READINGS:

- Daniel 5
- Psalms 62:9-12
- 1 Peter 5:5-6

Questions? Learnings? Praises? Prayers? To Do's? Jesus is...?

DATE:

214 READING

DANIEL AND LION'S DEN — DANIEL PRAYS THREE TIMES A DAY AND LIVES BLAMELESSLY

Daniel pictured Jesus. Like Jesus, he was the best leader in the kingdom. Like Jesus, he only could be accused of his relationship with God. Daniel disobeyed the government when they banned prayer. You also should disobey the government if they try to force you to disobey God. Ultimately God delivered Daniel from the lions to show His power, glory, and love to the world.

> *Now when Daniel knew that the writing [banning prayer] was signed, he went home. And in his upper room, with his windows open toward Jerusalem, he knelt down on his knees three times that day, and prayed and gave thanks before his God, as was his custom since early days. (Daniel 6:10)*

SCRIPTURE READINGS:

- Daniel 6
- Psalms 55:16-19
- 1 Peter 3:13-17

Questions? Learnings? Praises? Prayers? To Do's? Jesus is...?

DATE:

DANIEL AND THE FOUR BEASTS — THE SON OF MAN'S (I.E. JESUS') COMING AND HIS KINGDOM

Daniel dreamed about four beasts that pictured four coming kingdoms. The fourth kingdom conquered the earth and persecuted the saints. Then God showed Daniel the end times: the Son of Man (Jesus) comes, the fourth kingdom is destroyed, and the saints receive God's kingdom. The end times are great news if you love Jesus. Do you look forward to Jesus' return?

Then they will see the Son of Man coming in the clouds with great power and glory. And then He will send His angels, and gather together His elect from the four winds, from the farthest part of earth to the farthest part of heaven. (Mark 13:26–27)

SCRIPTURE READINGS:

- Daniel 7
- Mark 13:21-27
- Mark 14:60-65

Questions? Learnings? Praises? Prayers? To Do's? Jesus is...?

DATE:

216 READING

DANIEL PRAYS FOR JERUSALEM — 70 YEARS, 70 WEEKS, AND THE ABOMINATION OF DESOLATION

Daniel read Jeremiah's prophecy about 70 years of exile for their sins. In brokenness, Daniel confessed their sins. When was the last time you, in brokenness, confessed your sins? Then God revealed "70 weeks" (70 sets of seven years). Jesus arrived after the 69th week. The 70th week will be a seven-year period of tribulation where a covenant is broken in the middle of it.

> *Then I [Daniel] set my face toward the Lord God to make request by prayer and supplications, with fasting, sackcloth, and ashes… "We have sinned and committed iniquity, we have done wickedly and rebelled, even by departing from Your precepts and Your judgments. (Daniel 9:3, 5)*

SCRIPTURE READINGS:

- Daniel 9
- Jeremiah 25:8-14
- Matthew 24:3-27

Questions? Learnings? Praises? Prayers? To Do's? Jesus is…?

DATE:

217
REFLECTION AND PRAYER

Look Back at Last Week — List what God did and what God taught you over the last week. This is your "thank God list" for next week.

Look Forward to Next Week — List what events, decisions, deadlines, or progress needs to happen in the next week. This is your prayer list for next week.

DATE:

218 READING

DANIEL AND GABRIEL'S VISIT RE: PERSIA AND GREECE — MICHAEL THE ARCHANGEL

Daniel had another vision and started praying. After three weeks, Gabriel arrived and said, "Do not fear." Are you living in fear? Fear is often the sin of doubting God's power or love for you. Gabriel said God sent him the day Daniel prayed but the angelic representative of Persia delayed him. Jesus hears you when you pray too and is at work even when you don't see it yet.

> *Then he said to me, "Do not fear, Daniel, for from the first day that you set your heart to understand, and to humble yourself before your God, your words were heard; and I have come because of your words." (Daniel 10:12)*

SCRIPTURE READINGS:

- Daniel 10
- Revelation 12:7-9
- Daniel 12

Questions? Learnings? Praises? Prayers? To Do's? Jesus is...?

DATE:

EZEKIEL — EZEKIEL GRIEVES IN CAPTIVITY AND GOD'S CALL TO PREACH TO THE DISOBEDIENT CAPTIVES

Even in exile, the Jews continued to rebel against God. God told Ezekiel to share His message whether the people obeyed or not. Do you realize you're only responsible for how you follow Jesus? Not what others do? The people enjoyed listening to Ezekiel's messages but didn't change. Ezekiel pictured Jesus: a Spirit-filled Priest and Prophet sent to a rebellious Israel.

*You shall speak My words to them,
whether they hear or whether they refuse,
for they are rebellious. (Ezekiel 2:7)*

SCRIPTURE READINGS:

- Ezekiel 1:1-3
- Ezekiel 2
- Ezekiel 33:30-33

Questions? Learnings? Praises? Prayers? To Do's? Jesus is...?

DATE:

220 READING

EZEKIEL — EZEKIEL GRIEVES WITH THE CAPTIVES BUT DOES NOT GRIEVE THE LOSS OF HIS WIFE

Ezekiel was taken into captivity with the second group of Jews. Though the exiles were sad, they were still arrogant because their beloved Jerusalem wasn't destroyed. Are you trusting in something besides Jesus? God revealed to the Jews that, hundreds of miles away, Jerusalem was under siege. God was burning away the sins of Jerusalem like Ezekiel boiling meat.

> 'Speak to the house of Israel, "Thus says the Lord God: 'Behold, I will profane My sanctuary [the Jewish temple in Jerusalem], your arrogant boast, the desire of your eyes, the delight of your soul; and your sons and daughters whom you left behind shall fall by the sword. (Ezekiel 24:21)

SCRIPTURE READINGS:

- Ezekiel 3:1-15
- Psalms 137
- Ezekiel 24

Questions? Learnings? Praises? Prayers? To Do's? Jesus is...?

DATE:

EZEKIEL — BEING A FAITHFUL WATCHMAN FOR GOD AND BEING INNOCENT OF PEOPLE'S BLOOD

God made Ezekiel a watchman. If Ezekiel shared God's word and was ignored, their blood was on them. If Ezekiel withheld God's word and they died, he was accountable for their death. Paul referenced this, saying, "I am pure from the blood of all men." If you have Jesus, you have the message people need: Jesus. Ask God now who He wants you to share Jesus with. Listen. Go.

"So you, son of man: I have made you a watchman for the house of Israel; therefore you shall hear a word from My mouth and warn them for Me." (Ezekiel 33:7)

SCRIPTURE READINGS:

- Ezekiel 3:16-27
- Ezekiel 33:1-20
- Acts 20:25-27

Questions? Learnings? Praises? Prayers? To Do's? Jesus is...?

DATE:

222 READING

EZEKIEL — ISRAEL'S SINFUL HISTORY AND THEIR (NATIONAL AND INDIVIDUAL) RESURRECTION

God showed Israel grace by loving them, choosing them, and delivering them from Egypt. Israel responded by rebelling until they were destroyed. God showed Israel grace again by promising to resurrect their nation. Jesus promises to resurrect people too. If you have Jesus, you'll never die. Do you fear death or look forward to life after death? Jesus is the resurrection and the life.

> *Jesus said to her [Martha], "I am the resurrection and the life. He who believes in Me, though he may die, he shall live. And whoever lives and believes in Me shall never die. Do you believe this?" (John 11:25–26)*

SCRIPTURE READINGS:

- Ezekiel 20:1-38
- Ezekiel 37
- John 11:21-27

Questions? Learnings? Praises? Prayers? To Do's? Jesus is...?

DATE:

ESTHER — ESTHER BECOMES QUEEN AND MORDECAI PROTECTS THE KING

Esther and Mordecai were taken to Babylon with the second group of exiles. False prophets predicted a quick return. God told them to stay and bless their city. Are you blessing your city? Esther pictured you as a captive (you were captive to sin) who married the king (Christians are the bride of Christ). Are you a Christian? Are you thankful for how much Jesus blessed you?

And seek the peace of the city where I have caused you to be carried away captive, and pray to the Lord for it; for in its peace you will have peace. (Jeremiah 29:7)

SCRIPTURE READINGS:

- Esther 1
- Esther 2
- Jeremiah 29:1-11

Questions? Learnings? Praises? Prayers? To Do's? Jesus is…?

DATE:

224
REFLECTION AND PRAYER

Look Back at Last Week — List what God did and what God taught you over the last week. This is your "thank God list" for next week.

Look Forward to Next Week — List what events, decisions, deadlines, or progress needs to happen in the next week. This is your prayer list for next week.

DATE:

ESTHER — HAMAN'S PLOT AGAINST THE JEWS AND ESTHER'S COURAGEOUS RISK TO SEE THE KING

Queen Esther faced a decision. Would she stay quiet and hope God used someone else? Or risk her life for others by entering the king's presence without being asked? Esther asked others to fast and pray with her then stepped out in faith. Faith requires risk. You cannot live by faith without taking a risk for Jesus. Is the Holy Spirit prompting you to step out in faith? Do it today.

225 READING

> And Mordecai told them to answer Esther: "Do not think in your heart that you will escape in the king's palace any more than all the other Jews. For if you remain completely silent at this time, relief and deliverance will arise... you and your father's house will perish. Yet who knows whether you have come to the kingdom for such a time as this?" (Esther 4:13-14)

SCRIPTURE READINGS:

- Esther 3
- Esther 4
- Proverbs 21:1

Questions? Learnings? Praises? Prayers? To Do's? Jesus is...?

DATE:

226 READING

ESTHER — ESTHER'S BANQUETS, MORDECAI'S HONORING, AND HAMAN'S DEATH

God answered their prayers. When Esther stepped out in faith, the king showed her mercy. Do you realize every leader's heart is in God's hand? The king made Haman honor Mordecai, the man he planned to murder. Then the king hanged Haman on his own gallows. Are you facing a situation beyond your control? Give it to Jesus in prayer. That's when people see Him at work.

> Now Harbonah, one of the eunuchs, said to the king, "Look! The gallows, fifty cubits high, which Haman made for Mordecai, who spoke good on the king's behalf, is standing at the house of Haman." Then the king said, "Hang him on it!" (Esther 7:9)

SCRIPTURE READINGS:

- Esther 5
- Esther 6
- Esther 7

Questions? Learnings? Praises? Prayers? To Do's? Jesus is...?

DATE:

ESTHER — THE KING'S DECREE, THE JEWS SAVED, AND THE FEAST OF PURIM

Haman legalized the murder of Jews on a date chosen by casting lots (or "purim"). Then God moved the king to let the Jews defend themselves. Today, Jews celebrate God's deliverance on the holiday of Purim. Do you still celebrate Jesus delivering you? In Esther's day, many people converted when they saw God work. Pause and ask Jesus to work and draw people to Him.

> *[Celebrate Purim] as the days on which the Jews had rest from their enemies, as the month which was turned from sorrow to joy for them, and from mourning to a holiday; that they should make them days of feasting and joy, of sending presents to one another and gifts to the poor. (Esther 9:22)*

SCRIPTURE READINGS:

- Esther 8
- Esther 9
- Esther 10

Questions? Learnings? Praises? Prayers? To Do's? Jesus is…?

DATE:

228 READING

KING CYRUS — CYRUS DOESN'T KNOW GOD BUT FULFILLS PROPHECY ABOUT REBUILDING THE TEMPLE

Just as Jeremiah predicted, the Jews spent 70 years in Babylon. Then Cyrus became king. Cyrus didn't know God but God moved him to let the Jews return and rebuild the temple. It was a miracle. Why does Jesus do miracles in our lives? He's showing you there's no other God. He wants the world to know there's no other God. In your life, how has Jesus shown He is God?

> *I am the Lord, and there is no other; There is no God besides Me. I will gird you [King Cyrus], though you have not known Me, That they may know from the rising of the sun to its setting That there is none besides Me. I am the Lord, and there is no other; (Isaiah 45:5-6)*

SCRIPTURE READINGS:

- Ezra 1
- 2 Chronicles 36:15-23
- Isaiah 45:1-7

Questions? Learnings? Praises? Prayers? To Do's? Jesus is...?

DATE:

ZERUBBABEL — THE FIRST RETURN OF PEOPLE FROM CAPTIVITY TO REBUILD THE TEMPLE

Zerubbabel led the first return of Jews to the Promised Land. Around 50,000 people felt like they were dreaming as they laughed and sang and praised God for all He was doing. That's what Jesus wants to do for you. He wants you to be so stunned by Him and His work that you can't help yourself. Has Jesus' love and goodness ever made you laugh and sing to Him with joy?

229 READING

When the Lord brought back the captivity of Zion, We were like those who dream. Then our mouth was filled with laughter, And our tongue with singing. Then they said among the nations, "The Lord has done great things for them." (Psalm 126:1-2)

SCRIPTURE READINGS:

- Ezra 2
- Jeremiah 29:10-14
- Psalms 126

Questions? Learnings? Praises? Prayers? To Do's? Jesus is...?

DATE:

230 READING

ZERUBBABEL — THE TEMPLE REBUILDING PROJECT IS STOPPED AND THE CHURCH IS A TEMPLE

The Jews rebuilding the temple pictured Jesus building His church. They started with the altar (the cross), laid the cornerstone (Jesus) and foundation (apostles and prophets), and built walls (every Christian). Enemies opposed them (world, flesh, and devil). Does the story of the Jews rebuilding the temple picture your story? Are you growing in Jesus and building His church?

> *Now, therefore, you are no longer strangers and foreigners, but fellow citizens with the saints and members of the household of God... in whom you also are being built together for a dwelling place of God in the Spirit. (Ephesians 2:19, 22)*

SCRIPTURE READINGS:

- Ezra 3
- Ezra 4
- Ephesians 2:19-22

Questions? Learnings? Praises? Prayers? To Do's? Jesus is...?

DATE:

231
REFLECTION AND PRAYER

Look Back at Last Week — List what God did and what God taught you over the last week. This is your "thank God list" for next week.

Look Forward to Next Week — List what events, decisions, deadlines, or progress needs to happen in the next week. This is your prayer list for next week.

DATE:

232 READING

HAGGAI AND ZECHARIAH — GOD USES HAGGAI AND ZECHARIAH TO RESTART THE TEMPLE REBUILDING PROJECT

The Jews started rebuilding the temple but let their enemies stop them. After 16 years of idleness, God sent the prophets Haggai and Zechariah to help them start again. The people claimed, "It's not time to build." God asked, "Is it time for you to live in your nice houses?" Jesus is building His Kingdom around the world. Are you building your life or the kingdom of God?

> *Thus speaks the Lord of hosts, saying: "This people says, 'The time has not come, the time that the Lord's house should be built...' Is it time for you yourselves to dwell in your paneled houses, and this temple to lie in ruins?" (Haggai 1:2, 4)*

SCRIPTURE READINGS:

- Ezra 5:1-2
- Haggai 1
- Zechariah 1:1-6

Questions? Learnings? Praises? Prayers? To Do's? Jesus is...?

DATE:

ZERUBBABEL — THE JEWISH TEMPLE IS REBUILT JUST AS WISDOM BUILDS THE HOUSE

When people heard God's word, they started building again. Then the enemy tried to stop them again. Likewise when someone today starts to follow Jesus, the enemy opposes them. Life often gets harder. The Jews finished rebuilding because they were listening to God and God helped them. Jesus is a finisher and wants to help you finish God's will too. Are you listening?

So the elders of the Jews built, and they prospered through the prophesying of Haggai the prophet and Zechariah the son of Iddo. And they built and finished it, according to the commandment of the God of Israel, and according to the command of Cyrus, Darius, and Artaxerxes king of Persia. (Ezra 6:14)

SCRIPTURE READINGS:

- Ezra 5
- Ezra 6
- Proverbs 24:3-6

Questions? Learnings? Praises? Prayers? To Do's? Jesus is...?

DATE:

234 READING

EZRA — THE SECOND RETURN OF PEOPLE FROM CAPTIVITY TO REBUILD THE PEOPLE'S SPIRITUAL LIVES

After Zerubabbel rebuilt the temple, Ezra led 5,000 Jews back to rebuild Bible teaching. Ezra was a priest who prepared his heart to seek God's Law, do it, and teach others. Have you prepared your heart to learn the Bible, live it, and teach others to love and follow Jesus too? The spiritual state of Israel broke Ezra's heart. He fasted, prayed, and confessed their sins to God.

For Ezra had prepared his heart to seek the Law of the Lord, and to do it, and to teach statutes and ordinances in Israel. (Ezra 7:10)

SCRIPTURE READINGS:

- Ezra 7
- Ezra 8:21-36
- Ezra 9:1-11

Questions? Learnings? Praises? Prayers? To Do's? Jesus is...?

DATE:

NEHEMIAH — THE THIRD RETURN OF PEOPLE FROM CAPTIVITY TO REBUILD JERUSALEM'S WALLS AND PRAYER

In captivity, Nehemiah was the king's wine steward. Then he heard about Jerusalem in ruins. The king asked why he was sad. Nehemiah silently prayed and shared why. Long prayers don't impress Jesus. He knows what you need before you ask. The king let Nehemiah lead the third return of Jews from Babylon. Pour out your heart to Jesus. Tell Him what you need. He knows.

235
READING

And when you pray, do not use vain repetitions as the heathen do. For they think that they will be heard for their many words. Therefore do not be like them. For your Father knows the things you have need of before you ask Him. (Matthew 6:7-8)

SCRIPTURE READINGS:

- Nehemiah 1
- Nehemiah 2
- Matthew 6:7-8

Questions? Learnings? Praises? Prayers? To Do's? Jesus is...?

DATE:

236 READING

NEHEMIAH — REBUILDING JERUSALEM'S WALLS AND WALLS AS A SYMBOL OF EMOTIONAL CONTROL

Nehemiah gave each family a different section of the wall to repair. Nehemiah pictured Jesus who gives each Christian different spiritual gifts to build His church (1 Corinthians 12). What are your spiritual gifts? When Israel was threatened, they built with one hand and held a weapon with the other. Jesus said making disciples is like that: building and waging war (Luke 14).

> *Those who built on the wall, and those who carried burdens, loaded themselves so that with one hand they worked at construction, and with the other held a weapon. (Nehemiah 4:17)*

SCRIPTURE READINGS:

- Nehemiah 3
- Nehemiah 4
- Proverbs 25:28

Questions? Learnings? Praises? Prayers? To Do's? Jesus is...?

DATE:

NEHEMIAH — NEHEMIAH EXPERIENCES OPPOSITION AND NEEDS STRONG HANDS TO CONTINUE

Nehemiah faced continual opposition as the Jews rebuilt the walls: disobedience, distractions, accusations, fear. Have you experienced attacks like these as you and others build yourselves in Christ and build healthy boundaries in your lives? When Nehemiah asked God to strengthen his hands, God answered. They built the walls in 52 days. Ask Jesus to strengthen your hands.

237 READING

> Then I sent to him, saying, "No such things as you say are being done, but you invent them in your own heart." For they all were trying to make us afraid, saying, "Their hands will be weakened in the work, and it will not be done." Now therefore, O God, strengthen my hands. (Nehemiah 6:8-9)

SCRIPTURE READINGS:

- Nehemiah 5
- Nehemiah 6
- Zechariah 8:7-15

Questions? Learnings? Praises? Prayers? To Do's? Jesus is...?

DATE:

238
REFLECTION AND PRAYER

Look Back at Last Week — List what God did and what God taught you over the last week. This is your "thank God list" for next week.

Look Forward to Next Week — List what events, decisions, deadlines, or progress needs to happen in the next week. This is your prayer list for next week.

DATE:

EZRA — EZRA READS THE LAW TO THE PEOPLE AND THE BENEFITS OF BIBLE READING

God told the priests to read the law to Israel every seven years. Ezra did that. God's words helped His people fear Him, obey Him, and teach their kids. Jesus does the same with you. God's word is alive and powerful (Hebrews 4). He will use His Word to reveal Himself to you and transform your mind and heart. Are you as committed to Bible reading as your daily food?

239

READING

Gather the people together, men and women and little ones, and the stranger who is within your gates, that they may hear and that they may learn to fear the Lord your God and carefully observe all the words of this law, (Deuteronomy 31:12)

SCRIPTURE READINGS:

- Nehemiah 8
- Nehemiah 9
- Deuteronomy 31:9-13

Questions? Learnings? Praises? Prayers? To Do's? Jesus is...?

DATE:

240 READING

MALACHI — THE FINAL OLD TESTAMENT PROPHET (400+ YEARS BEFORE CHRIST) AND PROPHECIES OF CHRIST

Because Israel questioned God's love (Malachi 1:2), they stopped serving, giving, and being faithful in marriage. God sent Malachi to say, "Return to Me." Do you need to return to God? God's last words before 400 years of silence were about Jesus. At His first coming, Jesus was the "Messenger of the covenant." At His second coming, He will be the "Sun of righteousness."

> *But to you who fear My name The Sun of Righteousness [Jesus] shall arise With healing in His wings; And you shall go out And grow fat like stall-fed calves. (Malachi 4:2)*

SCRIPTURE READINGS:

- Malachi 2:7-17
- Malachi 3
- Malachi 4

Questions? Learnings? Praises? Prayers? To Do's? Jesus is...?

DATE:

JESUS' PREDECESSOR — JOHN THE BAPTIST'S CONCEPTION AND BIRTH

God sent John the Baptist to prepare Israel for Jesus. God started with John the Baptist's dad. Zacharias prayed for a child. When he didn't believe when God said yes, God took his ability to speak. When John was born, Zacharias was healed of unbelief and praised God. His heart was now prepared for Jesus. Are you preparing your heart every day to be receptive to Jesus?

241 READING

And the angel answered and said to him, "I am Gabriel, who stands in the presence of God, and was sent to speak to you and bring you these glad tidings. But behold, you will be mute and not able to speak until the day these things take place, because you did not believe my words which will be fulfilled in their own time." (Luke 1:19–20)

SCRIPTURE READINGS:

- Luke 1:1-25
- Luke 1:57-80
- Malachi 4:5-6

Questions? Learnings? Praises? Prayers? To Do's? Jesus is…?

DATE:

242 READING

JESUS' CONCEPTION — THE MIRACLE THAT A VIRGIN COULD CONCEIVE A CHILD BY THE HOLY SPIRIT

Before time began, Jesus existed as the Word; fully God. Then Jesus created the universe. At His birth, God clothed Himself in flesh. God told Mary that, while a virgin, she would give birth to God the Son and name Him Jesus. Mary believed God. Do you believe that nothing is impossible for God? Mary responded by rejoicing in Jesus. God was coming to be her Savior.

> *[Elizabeth said,] "Blessed is she who believed, for there will be a fulfillment of those things which were told her from the Lord." And Mary said: "My soul magnifies the Lord, And my spirit has rejoiced in God my Savior." (Luke 1:45–47)*

SCRIPTURE READINGS:

- Luke 1:26-56
- John 1:1-14
- 1 John 1:1-5

Questions? Learnings? Praises? Prayers? To Do's? Jesus is…?

DATE:

JESUS' GESTATION — MARY'S PREGNANCY AND JOSEPH'S CRISIS ("HOW SHOULD I DIVORCE MARY?")

243 READING

Joseph faced a difficult decision. His fiancée was pregnant and the baby wasn't his. Mary claimed to be a virgin pregnant with the Son of God. Joseph debated divorcing her publicly or privately. When people hurt you, do you shame them publicly or handle it with grace? God said to marry her and name the baby Jesus. Joseph obeyed God despite what others likely thought.

> *Therefore the Lord Himself will give you a sign: Behold, the virgin shall conceive and bear a Son, and shall call His name Immanuel. (Isaiah 7:14)*

SCRIPTURE READINGS:

- Matthew 1:18-25
- Deuteronomy 24:1-4
- Isaiah 7:13-14

Questions? Learnings? Praises? Prayers? To Do's? Jesus is...?

DATE:

244 READING

JESUS' BIRTH — JESUS' BIRTH, PROMISE, CIRCUMCISION, AND THE MYSTERY OF GODLINESS

Mary was about to give birth in the wrong city. The Ruler of Israel was to be from Bethlehem (Micah 5:2). God used a census to move Mary so Jesus was born in Bethlehem. God was fulfilling His word. When the shepherds saw Jesus, they were changed. They started telling people about Jesus and giving God the glory. Who is the last person you told about Jesus?

Now when they [the shepherds] had seen Him [Jesus], they made widely known the saying which was told them concerning this Child. (Luke 2:17)

SCRIPTURE READINGS:

- Luke 2:1-40
- Isaiah 9:6-7
- 1 Timothy 3:16

Questions? Learnings? Praises? Prayers? To Do's? Jesus is...?

DATE:

245
REFLECTION AND PRAYER

Look Back at Last Week — List what God did and what God taught you over the last week. This is your "thank God list" for next week.

Look Forward to Next Week — List what events, decisions, deadlines, or progress needs to happen in the next week. This is your prayer list for next week.

DATE:

246 READING

JESUS' CHILDHOOD — THE WISE MEN VISIT, JESUS IS TAKEN TO EGYPT, AND JESUS AT 12 YEARS OLD

Wise men asked where the King of the Jews was. Herod was worried. That was his title. The wise men left to worship Jesus. Wise people still do today. Are you wise? God protected Jesus from Herod until He grew up in Nazareth. By the age of 12, Jesus knew God was His real Dad. Jesus submitted to his mom and step-dad and grew. Jesus leads you to submit and grow too.

> *Then He went down with them and came to Nazareth, and was subject to them, but His mother kept all these things in her heart. And Jesus increased in wisdom and stature, and in favor with God and men. (Luke 2:51–52)*

SCRIPTURE READINGS:

- Matthew 2
- Micah 5:2-5
- Luke 2:41-52

Questions? Learnings? Praises? Prayers? To Do's? Jesus is…?

DATE:

JESUS' BAPTISM — JOHN THE BAPTIST'S MINISTRY AND HONOR OF BAPTIZING JESUS

John the Baptist pointed people to Jesus. Who are you pointing to Jesus these days? John said Jesus would give His people the Holy Spirit and burn God's enemies with fire. In response, people turned to God, confessed their sins, and were baptized. When people fully turn to God, they aren't afraid to show it. Then Jesus was baptized and God said He was very pleased.

> *And the Holy Spirit descended in bodily form like a dove upon Him, and a voice came from heaven which said, "You are My beloved Son; in You I am well pleased." (Luke 3:22)*

SCRIPTURE READINGS:

- Matthew 3
- Luke 3:1-23
- Isaiah 40:3-5

Questions? Learnings? Praises? Prayers? To Do's? Jesus is…?

DATE:

248 READING

JESUS' TEMPTATION — A 40-DAY FAST, THE BIBLE, AND THREE TYPES OF TEMPTATION (FLESH/EYES/PRIDE)

Before Jesus' public ministry, the devil tempted Him to sin: turn stones into bread, look at the world's kingdoms, and jump off a roof. You are tempted with the flesh, eyes, and pride too. Pause to thank Jesus that He didn't sin. Jesus resisted temptation by loving God more, rejecting any lies, and quoting the Bible. If Jesus is in you, He'll help you resist temptation that way too.

> *But He answered and said, "It is written, 'Man shall not live by bread alone, but by every word that proceeds from the mouth of God.' " (Matthew 4:4)*

SCRIPTURE READINGS:

- Matthew 4:1-11
- Deuteronomy 8:1-3
- 1 John 2:15-16

Questions? Learnings? Praises? Prayers? To Do's? Jesus is…?

DATE:

JESUS' FIRST DISCIPLES — JOHN THE BAPTIST POINTS PEOPLE TO JESUS THE LAMB OF GOD

249 READING

John the Baptist knew God called him to preach in the wilderness and prepare Israel for the Messiah. John didn't realize his cousin Jesus was Messiah until the Holy Spirit descended on Him. Then John said Jesus was the "Lamb of God" whose death would take away the sin of the world. Do you realize Jesus' sacrifice at the cross is the only way you can be forgiven of sin?

> *knowing that you were not redeemed with corruptible things, like silver or gold, from your aimless conduct received by tradition from your fathers, but with the precious blood of Christ, as of a lamb without blemish and without spot. (1 Peter 1:18–19)*

SCRIPTURE READINGS:

- John 1:15-51
- Deuteronomy 18:15-19
- 1 Peter 1:18-19

Questions? Learnings? Praises? Prayers? To Do's? Jesus is...?

DATE:

250 READING

JESUS' FIRST MIRACLE — A WEDDING RUNS OUT OF WINE (I.E. JOY) AND JESUS TURNS WATER TO WINE

Jesus' first miracle pictured the miracle He wants to do through you. The wine ran out (this world's joy). He chose empty vessels (people), filled them with water (Bible and Spirit), and turned water to wine (the miracle of Jesus' joy in you). He sent the servants (you) out to the people (who need Jesus). Are you experiencing the miracle of taking Jesus' joy to the world?

This beginning of signs Jesus did in Cana of Galilee, and manifested His glory; and His disciples believed in Him. (John 2:11)

SCRIPTURE READINGS:

- John 2:1-12
- Isaiah 24:11
- John 13:1

Questions? Learnings? Praises? Prayers? To Do's? Jesus is...?

DATE:

JESUS' PASSOVER AT JERUSALEM — CLEANSING THE TEMPLE, NICODEMUS, AND BEING BORN AGAIN

Nicodemus was a good religious leader who didn't understand the term "born again." Your first birth made you alive physically. Being born again makes you alive spiritually. How are you born again? The Holy Spirit moves and brings the seed of the word of God into your heart. When you believe in Jesus, you're born again. Have you made Jesus your Lord? Are you born again?

Jesus answered and said to him, "Most assuredly, I say to you, unless one is born again, he cannot see the kingdom of God." (John 3:3)

SCRIPTURE READINGS:

- John 2:13-25
- John 3:1-21
- 1 Peter 1:23

Questions? Learnings? Praises? Prayers? To Do's? Jesus is...?

DATE:

252
REFLECTION AND PRAYER

Look Back at Last Week — List what God did and what God taught you over the last week. This is your "thank God list" for next week.

Look Forward to Next Week — List what events, decisions, deadlines, or progress needs to happen in the next week. This is your prayer list for next week.

DATE:

JESUS' MINISTRY GROWS — JESUS' BAPTISMS GROW AND THE SAMARITAN WOMAN AT THE WELL

Jesus showed God's love for you and the world when he loved the woman at the well. She was a Samaritan (hated by the Jews), had a history with men (immoral), and fetched water when no one else was there (alone). Jesus knew all about her yet came and offered her eternal life. Jesus knows all about you too. Do you realize how great His love is for offering you eternal life?

253 READING

He who believes in the Son has everlasting life; and he who does not believe the Son shall not see life, but the wrath of God abides on him." (John 3:36)

SCRIPTURE READINGS:

- John 3:22-36
- John 4:1-42
- 2 Kings 17:24-41

Questions? Learnings? Praises? Prayers? To Do's? Jesus is...?

DATE:

254 READING

JESUS' SECOND MIRACLE — JESUS HEALS THE NOBLEMAN'S SON AND NAZARETH REJECTS JESUS

A nobleman begged Jesus to heal his son 20 miles away. Jesus did. When you pray, Jesus can change things miles away. The nobleman wasn't with his son but believed Jesus' word. Do you believe Jesus' word when you can't see it yet? Later, those in Jesus' hometown tried to murder Him when He noted God sometimes reached Gentiles (a widow and Namaan) instead of Jews.

> *"The Spirit of the Lord is upon Me, Because He has anointed Me To preach the gospel to the poor; He has sent Me to heal the brokenhearted, To proclaim liberty to the captives And recovery of sight to the blind, To set at liberty those who are oppressed; (Luke 4:18)*

SCRIPTURE READINGS:

- John 4:43-54
- Luke 4:14-30
- Isaiah 61:1-3

Questions? Learnings? Praises? Prayers? To Do's? Jesus is...?

DATE:

JESUS' HEALING IN JERUSALEM — JESUS HEALS AT A FEAST AND CLAIMS TO BE GOD

The Jews tried to kill Jesus because He kept saying He is God. Jesus said He is equal to God, is the "I AM" (Exodus 3), existed before Abraham, and is one with the Father. Jesus noted other witnesses to His deity too: John the Baptist, Jesus' works, God the Father, and the Scriptures. Do you believe the truth that Jesus is Almighty God clothed in human flesh?

255 READING

Jesus said to them, "Most assuredly, I say to you, before Abraham was, I AM." Then they took up stones to throw at Him; but Jesus hid Himself and went out of the temple, going through the midst of them, and so passed by. (John 8:58–59)

SCRIPTURE READINGS:

- John 5
- John 8:56-59
- John 10:29-33

Questions? Learnings? Praises? Prayers? To Do's? Jesus is…?

DATE:

256 READING

JESUS' MINISTRY AT CAPERNAUM — JOHN THE BAPTIST IS JAILED AND JESUS HEALS PEOPLE

After John the Baptist was jailed, Jesus made Capernaum (the region of Zebulun and Naphtali) his ministry base. He drew crowds by healing people then preached the kingdom of God. That's what Jesus wants to do through you too. Jesus wants to draw people by His love as you serve them. Then Jesus wants you to tell them the good news about Him and the kingdom of God.

> *Now when it was day, He departed and went into a deserted place. And the crowd sought Him and came to Him, and tried to keep Him from leaving them; but He said to them, "I must preach the kingdom of God to the other cities also, because for this purpose I have been sent." (Luke 4:42–43)*

SCRIPTURE READINGS:

- Matthew 4:12-17
- Isaiah 9:1-2
- Luke 4:31-44

Questions? Learnings? Praises? Prayers? To Do's? Jesus is…?

DATE:

JESUS' DISCIPLES CALLED — JESUS CALLS PEOPLE TO BEGIN FOLLOWING HIM

As Jesus ministered in Galilee, multitudes started following Him. Then He called individuals to follow Him (four fishermen and a hated tax collector). Their call pictured your call. They were (1) broken over their sinfulness (Peter), (2) stunned by Jesus' power (fishermen), (3) shocked Jesus was with them (Matthew), (4) leaving all to follow Him. Pray those four things to Jesus.

257
READING

Then He said to them, "Follow Me, and I will make you fishers of men." (Matthew 4:19)

SCRIPTURE READINGS:

- Matthew 4:18-25
- Luke 5:1-11
- Matthew 9:9-13

Questions? Learnings? Praises? Prayers? To Do's? Jesus is…?

DATE:

258 READING

JESUS' HEALINGS IN CAPERNAUM — JESUS HEALS A LEPER AND A PARALYTIC IS LOWERED THROUGH A ROOF

As Jesus healed people, He sent them to the priests. God intended the stream of healed people to alert them to the Messiah. Jesus became so busy that He woke up early to talk with God. How are you getting alone to talk with God? Four men lowered a paralyzed friend to Jesus through a roof. Sometimes it takes an entire group of friends to bring someone to Jesus.

And He charged him to tell no one, "But go and show yourself to the priest, and make an offering for your cleansing, as a testimony to them, just as Moses commanded." (Luke 5:14)

SCRIPTURE READINGS:

- Luke 5:12-26
- Mark 1:32-45
- Mark 2:1-12

Questions? Learnings? Praises? Prayers? To Do's? Jesus is...?

DATE:

259
REFLECTION AND PRAYER

Look Back at Last Week — List what God did and what God taught you over the last week. This is your "thank God list" for next week.

Look Forward to Next Week — List what events, decisions, deadlines, or progress needs to happen in the next week. This is your prayer list for next week.

DATE:

260 READING

JESUS' MINISTRY TO SINNERS — JESUS EATS WITH SINNERS AND FORGIVES THEM

When Jesus ate with sinners, religious people complained. Do you make time to eat with people far from God? When Jesus let a sinful woman kiss and worship at His feet, a Pharisee criticized. Jesus told a story of two debtors. Which debtor are you? If you think Jesus forgave you a little, you'll love Jesus a little. If you think Jesus forgave you of countless sins, you'll love Jesus a lot.

Therefore I say to you, her sins, which are many, are forgiven, for she loved much. But to whom little is forgiven, the same loves little." (Luke 7:47)

SCRIPTURE READINGS:

- Luke 5:29-32
- Luke 7:36-50
- Luke 18:9-14

Questions? Learnings? Praises? Prayers? To Do's? Jesus is…?

DATE:

JESUS' CHOOSING OF THE 12 — JESUS PRAYS ALL NIGHT, CHOOSES 12 APOSTLES, AND IS CRITICIZED BY FAMILY

The 12 apostles didn't volunteer. Jesus chose them. (If you know Jesus, He chose you too.) Choosing the 12 was so important that Jesus prayed all night for wisdom. The other time Jesus prayed all night was before the cross. After choosing the 12, Jesus spent three years equipping them to love God, love each other, and bear fruit. Is Jesus growing you those three ways too?

261 READING

> *Now it came to pass in those days that He went out to the mountain to pray, and continued all night in prayer to God. And when it was day, He called His disciples to Himself; and from them He chose twelve whom He also named apostles: (Luke 6:12–13)*

SCRIPTURE READINGS:

- Luke 6:1-16
- Mark 3:1-21
- John 15:12-17

Questions? Learnings? Praises? Prayers? To Do's? Jesus is...?

DATE:

262 READING

JESUS' SERMON ON THE MOUNT — THE BEATITUDES, KINGDOM-LIFE, AND JESUS FULFILLING THE SCRIPTURES

In the Sermon on the Mount, Jesus lifted up God's kingdom and exposed all self-righteousness. The rich aren't blessed, the poor are. Hate is murder in your heart. Lay up treasures in heaven, not on earth. The Sermon on the Mount shows God's perfection. It's impossible without Jesus. Jesus fulfilled the Law for us. He gives His children His Holy Spirit. Do you have the Holy Spirit?

Let your light so shine before men, that they may see your good works and glorify your Father in heaven. (Matthew 5:16)

SCRIPTURE READINGS:

- Matthew 5
- Matthew 6
- Luke 6:17-49

Questions? Learnings? Praises? Prayers? To Do's? Jesus is...?

DATE:

JESUS' HEALINGS IN CAPERNAUM AND NAIN — THE SERVANT, THE WIDOW'S SON, AND PETER'S MOTHER

263 READING

Jesus healed people because He cared for them: the Centurion's servant, the widow's son, Peter's mother-in-law. Jesus cares about you too. Jesus' healings fulfilled Isaiah's prophecy about the One who heals. His healings also pictured how He wants to heal you spiritually. Healing the blind pictured giving you spiritual sight. Pause and pray for Jesus to heal people.

And when He came near the gate of the city, behold, a dead man was being carried out, the only son of his mother; and she was a widow. And a large crowd from the city was with her. When the Lord saw her, He had compassion on her and said to her, "Do not weep." (Luke 7:12–13)

SCRIPTURE READINGS:

- Luke 7:1-16
- Matthew 8:5-17
- Isaiah 53:4

Questions? Learnings? Praises? Prayers? To Do's? Jesus is…?

DATE:

264 READING

JESUS' DEMANDS OF DISCIPLESHIP — TO FOLLOW JESUS IS TO MAKE HIM YOUR FIRST PRIORITY

The call to follow Jesus is the end of "me first." If you follow Jesus, you surrender all rights to Him out of deep love and gratitude. What about me first living where I want? What about me first going to the one year anniversary of my dad's death? What about me first saying goodbye? You can't follow Jesus without His cross. Have you ended "me first" by picking up your cross today?

> *Then Jesus said to His disciples, "If anyone desires to come after Me, let him deny himself, and take up his cross, and follow Me. (Matthew 16:24)*

SCRIPTURE READINGS:

- Matthew 8:18-22
- Luke 9:43-62
- Matthew 16:24-26

Questions? Learnings? Praises? Prayers? To Do's? Jesus is...?

DATE:

JOHN THE BAPTIST'S DOUBTS — JOHN QUESTIONS JESUS FROM PRISON AND JESUS COMMENTS ON JOHN

As John the Baptist sat in jail, his doubts grew. "How could Jesus let this happen? Isn't He the Son of God?" He sent messengers to check. Have you questioned God in your suffering? Jesus let the messengers watch Him then sent them back. Then Jesus compared His generation to immature, controlling children who said John was too ascetic and Jesus was too social.

> Jesus answered and said to them, "Go and tell John the things you have seen and heard: that the blind see, the lame walk, the lepers are cleansed, the deaf hear, the dead are raised, the poor have the gospel preached to them. (Luke 7:22)

SCRIPTURE READINGS:

- Luke 7:18-35
- Matthew 11
- Isaiah 35:3-6

Questions? Learnings? Praises? Prayers? To Do's? Jesus is...?

DATE:

266
REFLECTION AND PRAYER

Look Back at Last Week — List what God did and what God taught you over the last week. This is your "thank God list" for next week.

Look Forward to Next Week — List what events, decisions, deadlines, or progress needs to happen in the next week. This is your prayer list for next week.

DATE:

JESUS' MINISTRY AT SEA OF GALILEE — JESUS CALMS THE SEA AND CASTS OUT LEGION

One night, Jesus said, "Let us cross over to the other side." He promised that all would arrive. In the storm, the disciples doubted. When He calmed the storm, He asked, "Do you have no faith?" Later Jesus healed a demon-possessed man who was cutting, crying, and uncontrollable. Jesus told him what He tells you. "Go home to your friends and share what God has done for you."

However, Jesus did not permit him, but said to him, "Go home to your friends, and tell them what great things the Lord has done for you, and how He has had compassion on you." And he departed and began to proclaim in Decapolis all that Jesus had done for him; and all marveled. (Mark 5:19–20)

SCRIPTURE READINGS:

- Luke 8:19-40
- Mark 4:35-41
- Mark 5:1-20

Questions? Learnings? Praises? Prayers? To Do's? Jesus is…?

DATE:

268 READING

JESUS' MINISTRY AT SEA OF GALILEE — JESUS HEALS A DAUGHTER AND A HEMORRHAGING WOMAN

Sometimes Jesus' interruptions were interrupted. A synagogue leader begged Jesus to heal his dying 12-year old daughter. On the way to heal the girl, a woman with a 12-year blood flow touched Jesus' garment and was healed. Then Jesus continued on and raised the girl from the dead. Do you trust Jesus enough to let Him interrupt your plans and schedules for Himself?

> *Then He said to His disciples, "The harvest truly is plentiful, but the laborers are few. Therefore pray the Lord of the harvest to send out laborers into His harvest." (Matthew 9:37–38)*

SCRIPTURE READINGS:

- Luke 8:41-56
- Mark 5:21-43
- Matthew 9:14-38

Questions? Learnings? Praises? Prayers? To Do's? Jesus is...?

DATE:

JESUS' SENDING OF THE 12 — JESUS PREPARES THE 12 FOR CONFLICT AND SENDS THEM OUT

Jesus trained His 12 apostles by teaching them and showing them how to minister. Then He sent them out in six groups of two to see which Jewish cities He should visit. When they went, they took no money and made no plans of where to stay (they lived by faith). Are you teaching Christians and showing them how to minister too? Are you telling non-Christians about Jesus?

269

READING

And He called the twelve to Himself, and began to send them out two by two, and gave them power over unclean spirits. (Mark 6:7)

SCRIPTURE READINGS:

- Matthew 10
- Micah 7:5-7
- Mark 6:7-13

Questions? Learnings? Praises? Prayers? To Do's? Jesus is...?

DATE:

270 READING

JESUS' "WORK" ON THE SABBATH — JESUS HEALS ON THE SABBATH AND THE UNPARDONABLE SIN

Jesus challenged Jewish teachings about Sabbath rest. His disciples plucked grains (but didn't harvest). He healed a man (but Jews helped animals). The Jews plotted to kill Jesus. Instead of fighting back, He withdrew. Do you fight back or let God fight for you? When the leaders said Jesus cast out demons by Satan, they rejected the Holy Spirit who was drawing them to Jesus.

> *But if you had known what this means, 'I desire mercy and not sacrifice,' you would not have condemned the guiltless. For the Son of Man is Lord even of the Sabbath." (Matthew 12:7–8)*

SCRIPTURE READINGS:

- Matthew 12
- Hosea 6:6
- Isaiah 42:1-4

Questions? Learnings? Praises? Prayers? To Do's? Jesus is...?

DATE:

JESUS' NEW TEACHING STYLE — AFTER ISRAEL'S REJECTION, JESUS STARTS TEACHING IN PARABLES

When the leaders of Israel officially rejected Jesus, He changed His teaching style to parables. His disciples asked why. Jesus gave two reasons: to hide truth from closed hearts and reveal truth to open hearts. The Bible is like seeds. Your heart is like soil. What is the state of your heart? (1) Blinded by Satan? (2) Unwilling to suffer? (3) Choked by sin? (4) Or open to Jesus?

271 READING

> *For the hearts of this people have grown dull. Their ears are hard of hearing, And their eyes they have closed, Lest they should see with their eyes and hear with their ears, Lest they should understand with their hearts and turn, So that I should heal them.' (Matthew 13:15)*

SCRIPTURE READINGS:

- Matthew 13
- Isaiah 6:8-10
- Psalms 78:1-4

Questions? Learnings? Praises? Prayers? To Do's? Jesus is...?

DATE:

272 READING

JOHN THE BAPTIST'S MURDER — HEROD BEHEADS JOHN THE BAPTIST FOR HIS WIFE, HERODIAS

Herod fell in love with his brother's wife Herodias. Then they divorced and married each other. John the Baptist preached that they broke Moses' law. Herod jailed him but Herodias wanted him dead. If you follow Jesus, do you expect to suffer persecution (2 Timothy 3:12)? Or, are you surprised when you suffer for Jesus? Later, Herodias tricked Herod into cutting off John's head.

Assuredly, I say to you, among those born of women there has not risen one greater than John the Baptist; but he who is least in the kingdom of heaven is greater than he. (Matthew 11:11)

SCRIPTURE READINGS:

- Matthew 14:1-12
- Mark 6:14-31
- Matthew 11:11-12

Questions? Learnings? Praises? Prayers? To Do's? Jesus is...?

DATE:

273
REFLECTION AND PRAYER

Look Back at Last Week — List what God did and what God taught you over the last week. This is your "thank God list" for next week.

Look Forward to Next Week — List what events, decisions, deadlines, or progress needs to happen in the next week. This is your prayer list for next week.

DATE:

274 READING

JESUS' BOAT TO CAPERNAUM — FEEDING THE 5000, WALKING ON WATER, AND THE BREAD OF LIFE

When Jesus tried to rest with His disciples, thousands followed Him. Jesus had compassion on them. He taught and miraculously fed 5,000 men (plus women and children). Then, He walked on water. Peter did too when he believed. The next day, Jesus said the bread pictured Him. Are you coming to Jesus to fulfill your hunger? In Him, you'll find joy, life, contentment, and rest.

And Jesus said to them, "I am the bread of life. He who comes to Me shall never hunger, and he who believes in Me shall never thirst. (John 6:35)

SCRIPTURE READINGS:

- Mark 6:30-56
- Matthew 14:13-36
- John 6

Questions? Learnings? Praises? Prayers? To Do's? Jesus is...?

DATE:

JESUS' CONFRONTATION OF THE PHARISEES — THE PHARISEES, A GREEK WOMAN, AND A DEAF-MUTE

The Jews criticized the disciples for not following their ritual hand washing tradition. Since the Jews were rejecting God's word to keep their tradition, God was rejecting their worship. Are you willing to follow God's word even when it breaks with tradition? Jesus said physical things don't defile you. Sinful thoughts do like evil, lust, murder, theft, greed, deceit, envy, slander, and pride.

275 READING

> And in vain they worship Me, Teaching as doctrines the commandments of men.' For laying aside the commandment of God, you hold the tradition of men—the washing of pitchers and cups, and many other such things you do." (Mark 7:7–8)

SCRIPTURE READINGS:

- Mark 7
- Matthew 15:1-31
- Isaiah 29:13-14

Questions? Learnings? Praises? Prayers? To Do's? Jesus is...?

DATE:

276 READING

JESUS' WARNING TO APOSTLES — FEEDING THE 4000, FALSE DOCTRINE, AND A TWO-PHASE HEALING

Jesus fed the 5,000 (plus women and children) and the 4,000. Then He warned His disciples about the leaven (yeast) of the Jewish leaders. He was warning them about false teaching. False teaching spreads like yeast and puffs you up with arrogance. Paul told Timothy how to avoid being deceived. Are you giving yourself consistently to Bible reading and Bible teaching?

> Then Jesus said to them, "Take heed and beware of the leaven of the Pharisees and the Sadducees."... Then they understood that He did not tell them to beware of the leaven of bread, but of the doctrine [teaching] of the Pharisees and Sadducees. (Matthew 16:6, 12)

SCRIPTURE READINGS:

- Mark 8:1-26
- Matthew 16:1-12
- 1 Timothy 4:13-16

Questions? Learnings? Praises? Prayers? To Do's? Jesus is...?

DATE:

JESUS' MINISTRY AT CAESAREA PHILIPPI — PETER'S CONFESSION AND THE PROMISE OF THE CHURCH

When Jesus asked His disciples who He was, Peter said, "You're the Messiah, the Son of God." Peter was blessed because only God can reveal that Jesus is the Son of God. Humans can't. Have you confessed Jesus Christ is the Son of God? If so, God Himself lives inside you. Jesus then revealed how He would spread this message to the world. Jesus would build His church.

Simon Peter answered and said, "You are the Christ, the Son of the living God." Jesus answered and said to him, "Blessed are you, Simon Bar-Jonah, for flesh and blood has not revealed this to you, but My Father who is in heaven. (Matthew 16:16–17)

SCRIPTURE READINGS:

- Matthew 16:13-28
- 1 John 4:14-16
- Philippians 2:5-11

Questions? Learnings? Praises? Prayers? To Do's? Jesus is…?

DATE:

278 READING

JESUS' TRANSFIGURATION — PETER'S EXPERIENCE ON THE MOUNTAIN AND HIS COMMENTS ON SCRIPTURE

At the Mount of Transfiguration, Peter, James, and John saw a bright cloud and Jesus shining with glory. They heard Jesus talk of His death and the Father say He was pleased. Later, Peter wrote that this moment built his faith in Jesus and Scripture. Do you realize the Bible is more reliable than any vision or voice you experience? Experiences can deceive. The Bible is sure.

> *for prophecy never came by the will of man, but holy men of God spoke as they were moved by the Holy Spirit. (2 Peter 1:21)*

SCRIPTURE READINGS:

- Matthew 17
- Luke 9:27-45
- 2 Peter 1:16-21

Questions? Learnings? Praises? Prayers? To Do's? Jesus is...?

DATE:

JESUS' ANSWERS TO DISCIPLES' QUESTIONS — JESUS ON CHILDREN, OFFENSES, AND FORGIVENESS

Jesus showed us God's love for children. When Jesus was asked who was greatest in God's kingdom, He called a child. Are you following Jesus with childlike faith? Jesus warned people not to offend or despise children. Jesus also interrupted adults for children. If Jesus is your Savior, you're a child of God. Are you humbling yourself before your loving Heavenly Dad?

> *and said, "Assuredly, I say to you, unless you are converted and become as little children, you will by no means enter the kingdom of heaven. (Matthew 18:3)*

SCRIPTURE READINGS:

- Matthew 18
- Psalm 131
- Deuteronomy 19:15

Questions? Learnings? Praises? Prayers? To Do's? Jesus is...?

DATE:

280
REFLECTION AND PRAYER

Look Back at Last Week — List what God did and what God taught you over the last week. This is your "thank God list" for next week.

Look Forward to Next Week — List what events, decisions, deadlines, or progress needs to happen in the next week. This is your prayer list for next week.

DATE:

JESUS' SENDING OF MORE DISCIPLES — SENDING 70+ MORE, THE GOOD SAMARITAN, AND MARY/MARTHA

Jesus added disciples when He called the 12. Jesus multiplied disciples when He sent the 12 to make disciples (six more groups of 12 would be 72). Jesus' goal is multiplication. Are you making disciples who make disciples? A disciple loves God like Mary (who spent time with Jesus). A disciple loves their neighbor like the Good Samaritan (who spent time to minister).

281
READING

After these things the Lord appointed seventy others also, and sent them two by two before His face into every city and place where He Himself was about to go. (Luke 10:1)

SCRIPTURE READINGS:

- Luke 10
- Matthew 9:35-38
- Matthew 6:25-34

Questions? Learnings? Praises? Prayers? To Do's? Jesus is...?

DATE:

282 READING

JESUS' MINISTRY AT THE FEAST OF TABERNACLES — ARRIVING SECRETLY AND THE WATER OF THE SPIRIT

Leaders in Judea wanted to kill Jesus and people were afraid to talk about Him. But when Jesus taught in the temple, more believed. Later Jesus said if you believe in Him, you'll receive the Holy Spirit flowing through you like rivers of living water. Does Jesus live inside you? Are you experiencing the life-giving flow of the Holy Spirit through you? Have you believed in Jesus?

> *He who believes in Me, as the Scripture has said, out of his heart will flow rivers of living water." But this He spoke concerning the Spirit, whom those believing in Him would receive; for the Holy Spirit was not yet given, because Jesus was not yet glorified. (John 7:38–39)*

SCRIPTURE READINGS:

- John 7
- Isaiah 44:1-8
- Isaiah 55

Questions? Learnings? Praises? Prayers? To Do's? Jesus is...?

DATE:

JESUS' MINISTRY IN JERUSALEM — THE WOMAN CAUGHT IN ADULTERY AND JESUS CLAIMS TO BE THE "I AM"

A mob brought a woman caught committing adultery to Jesus but let the man go free. Calmly, Jesus wrote on the ground. Then He said, "Let the one without sin throw the first stone." The mob left. Then Jesus told her, "I don't condemn you. Let's not do that again." How do you respond when people sin? Are you letting Jesus lead you to remain calm? Gracious? Hopeful?

283

READING

So when they continued asking Him, He raised Himself up and said to them, "He who is without sin among you, let him throw a stone at her first." (John 8:7)

SCRIPTURE READINGS:

- John 8
- John 3:16-21
- Exodus 3:13-15

Questions? Learnings? Praises? Prayers? To Do's? Jesus is…?

DATE:

284 READING

JESUS' MINISTRY IN JERUSALEM — HEALING A BLIND MAN, THE TRAGEDY AT SILOAM, AND SPIRITUAL BLINDNESS

Jesus said a man was born blind to reveal how God worked. Jesus made him eyes of clay (like creating Adam), anointed his eyes, and sent him to wash. He believed Jesus, went, and could see. The blind man pictured you when you were lost, born spiritually blind to the gospel. If you've believed in Jesus and can see, are you sharing the gospel with others so they can see?

> *But even if our gospel is veiled, it is veiled to those who are perishing, whose minds the god of this age has blinded, who do not believe, lest the light of the gospel of the glory of Christ, who is the image of God, should shine on them. (2 Corinthians 4:3-4)*

SCRIPTURE READINGS:

- John 9
- Luke 13:1-5
- 2 Corinthians 4:1-6

Questions? Learnings? Praises? Prayers? To Do's? Jesus is...?

DATE:

JESUS' MINISTRY AS THE GOOD SHEPHERD — JESUS THE GOOD SHEPHERD AND HIS SHEEP

Jesus said, "I am the door of the sheep." Jesus is the only entrance to God's flock. Have you entered God's family through Jesus? Jesus said, "I am the good shepherd." Israel's leaders had taken advantage of the flock. Is Jesus your shepherd? Is Jesus speaking to you, leading you, feeding you, and protecting you? Do you recognize Jesus' voice when He speaks to you?

> *I am the good shepherd. The good shepherd gives His life for the sheep… My sheep hear My voice, and I know them, and they follow Me. (John 10:11, 27)*

SCRIPTURE READINGS:

- John 10
- Ezekiel 34
- Isaiah 40:9-11

Questions? Learnings? Praises? Prayers? To Do's? Jesus is…?

DATE:

286 READING

JESUS' TEACHINGS ON PRAYER — THE LORD'S PRAYER, THE PERSISTENT FRIEND, AND GOD THE FATHER

After Jesus finished praying one day, a disciple asked Him to teach them how to pray. He taught them the Lord's Prayer. Jesus didn't say to mindlessly repeat it. He was giving a plan for prayer: praise God, then pray for God's will, today's needs, and forgiveness for all. Do you pray to God as if He's the best Dad possible? He is the best Dad. He created you for love and relationship.

> f you abide in Me, and My words abide in you, you will ask what you desire, and it shall be done for you. (John 15:7)

SCRIPTURE READINGS:

- Luke 11:1-13
- Matthew 6:5-14
- John 15:5-8

Questions? Learnings? Praises? Prayers? To Do's? Jesus is...?

DATE:

287

REFLECTION AND PRAYER

Look Back at Last Week — List what God did and what God taught you over the last week. This is your "thank God list" for next week.

Look Forward to Next Week — List what events, decisions, deadlines, or progress needs to happen in the next week. This is your prayer list for next week.

DATE:

288 READING

JESUS' STORIES ABOUT MONEY — DIVIDING THE INHERITANCE AND PEOPLE'S STRESS ABOUT MONEY

Why did Jesus talk more about money than heaven, hell, and faith combined? Money reveals your heart and Jesus wants your heart. When you give to God first, you show that you trust God and He's first in your heart. What is your giving revealing about your heart? When you grow in giving, God changes your heart too. Where your treasure is, there your heart will be also.

For where your treasure is, there your heart will be also. (Luke 12:34)

SCRIPTURE READINGS:

- Luke 12
- 1 Timothy 6:5-19
- Philippians 4:10-19

Questions? Learnings? Praises? Prayers? To Do's? Jesus is...?

DATE:

JESUS' TEACHINGS ON ISRAEL — THE PARABLE OF THE FIG TREE (I.E. ISRAEL) AND HEALING A CRIPPLED WOMAN

Jesus told a parable about a man planting a fig tree and seeking fruit for three years. Jesus planted Israel like a fig tree and sought fruit over His three years of ministry. The week Jesus died, He saw a fig tree with no fruit but covered with fig leaves like Adam and Eve in the garden. Fig trees picture you too (James 3:12). Is Jesus bearing fruit through you by His Holy Spirit?

> *He also spoke this parable: "A certain man had a fig tree planted in his vineyard, and he came seeking fruit on it and found none. (Luke 13:6)*

SCRIPTURE READINGS:

- Luke 13:6-35
- Mark 11:12-14
- Hosea 9:10

Questions? Learnings? Praises? Prayers? To Do's? Jesus is…?

DATE:

290 READING

JESUS' TEACHINGS AT A SABBATH MEAL — THE PARABLE OF THE SUPPER, PRIDE, AND HUMILITY

Jesus went to eat supper with a Pharisee on the Sabbath. The Pharisees were hypocrites who criticized Jesus for healing on the Sabbath when they'd help animals. The Pharisees also blindly rejected God's invitation to His kingdom supper someday. After supper, Jesus revealed the cost of being His disciple. Are you willing to forsake all that you have, even your own life, for Jesus?

> *And whoever does not bear his cross and come after Me cannot be My disciple… So likewise, whoever of you does not forsake all that he has cannot be My disciple. (Luke 14:27, 33)*

SCRIPTURE READINGS:

- Luke 14
- Proverbs 11:2
- Proverbs 25:6-7

Questions? Learnings? Praises? Prayers? To Do's? Jesus is…?

DATE:

JESUS' SEEKING OF THE LOST — SEEKING FOR PEOPLE LIKE SEEKING FOR SHEEP, COINS, AND A PRODIGAL SON

When the Jews complained about Jesus befriending sinners, He told three stories. Shepherds leave their flock to find one sheep that's lost. Women sweep their dirt floors to find one coin that's lost. Dads rejoice over a wayward son who returns after being lost. To Jesus, you're the lost sheep, lost coin, and lost son. Is Jesus moving you to pursue your lost friends like He does?

What man of you, having a hundred sheep, if he loses one of them, does not leave the ninety-nine in the wilderness, and go after the one which is lost until he finds it?... Or what woman, having ten silver coins, if she loses one coin, does not light a lamp, sweep the house, and search carefully until she finds it? (Luke 15:4, 8)

SCRIPTURE READINGS:

- Luke 15
- Jeremiah 50:6
- Psalms 119:174-176

Questions? Learnings? Praises? Prayers? To Do's? Jesus is…?

DATE:

292 READING

JESUS' STORIES ABOUT RICHES AND WISDOM — THE UNJUST STEWARD, THE RICH MAN, AND LAZARUS

Jesus said a rich man never helped a beggar named Lazarus. When they died, Lazarus went to rest while the rich man went to hell. The rich man begged for escape but his destiny was set. He begged for his brothers but the Bible was enough for them. Jesus died to deliver people from a hell God didn't create for them (Matthew 25:41). Do you live as if you believe hell is real?

But he said to him, 'If they do not hear Moses and the prophets, neither will they be persuaded though one rise from the dead.' " (Luke 16:31)

SCRIPTURE READINGS:

- Luke 16
- 1 Corinthians 4:1-5
- Deuteronomy 15:7-11

Questions? Learnings? Praises? Prayers? To Do's? Jesus is…?

DATE:

JESUS' TEACHINGS ON FORGIVENESS — JESUS TEACHES ON FORGIVENESS AND HEALS 10 LEPERS

Jesus' followers are very forgiving. We forgive people because Jesus forgave us and paid for their sins too. Have you forgiven someone seven times in one day? In Matthew 18, Jesus said to forgive 490 times. Another time, Jesus healed ten lepers. Nine went to the priests. Only one person turned around to thank Jesus and glorify God. Are you remembering to thank Jesus?

And if he sins against you seven times in a day, and seven times in a day returns to you, saying, 'I repent,' you shall forgive him." (Luke 17:4)

SCRIPTURE READINGS:

- Luke 17
- Proverbs 24:16
- Psalms 50:22-23

Questions? Learnings? Praises? Prayers? To Do's? Jesus is...?

DATE:

294
REFLECTION AND PRAYER

Look Back at Last Week — List what God did and what God taught you over the last week. This is your "thank God list" for next week.

Look Forward to Next Week — List what events, decisions, deadlines, or progress needs to happen in the next week. This is your prayer list for next week.

DATE:

JESUS' RAISING OF LAZARUS — JESUS RAISES LAZARUS AND THE PHARISEES PLOT JESUS' DEATH

Jesus understands being sad when someone dies. God in human form wept at the grave of His friend Lazarus. Jesus told Martha that, if you believe in Him, you don't die. You transition to being in God's presence after death. Then the Holy Spirit will raise your body someday like Lazarus. If you don't have the Holy Spirit, you're not a Christian. Do you have the Holy Spirit?

But if the Spirit of Him who raised Jesus from the dead dwells in you, He who raised Christ from the dead will also give life to your mortal bodies through His Spirit who dwells in you. (Romans 8:11)

SCRIPTURE READINGS:

- John 11
- John 12:9-11
- Romans 8:9-11

Questions? Learnings? Praises? Prayers? To Do's? Jesus is...?

DATE:

296 READING

JESUS' MINISTRY ACROSS THE JORDAN — MARRIAGE, THE RICH YOUNG RULER, AND SACRIFICES FOR GOD

When Jesus was asked about divorce, He shared God's vision for marriage from the beginning: one man and one woman for life. In Deuteronomy 24, God allowed divorce because of Israel's hard hearts. Another time, a rich young leader asked about eternal life. Since he trusted in his money, Jesus told him to give everything to the poor. Do you feel safer with money or God?

And He answered and said to them, "Have you not read that He who made them at the beginning 'made them male and female,' and said, 'For this reason a man shall leave his father and mother and be joined to his wife, and the two shall become one flesh'? (Matthew 19:4–5)

SCRIPTURE READINGS:

- Matthew 19
- Mark 10:1-30
- Luke 18:15-30

Questions? Learnings? Praises? Prayers? To Do's? Jesus is...?

DATE:

JESUS' FINAL TRIP TO JERUSALEM — THE PARABLE OF THE LABORERS AND THE RIGHT HAND OF JESUS

Jesus warned His disciples that, in Jerusalem, He would be betrayed, tortured, murdered, and rise again. James and John responded by asking for the two thrones beside Jesus. The others were upset, likely wishing they asked first. This world makes leadership about them. Jesus makes leadership about sacrificial service. Is Jesus leading you to give your life for others?

For even the Son of Man did not come to be served, but to serve, and to give His life a ransom for many." (Mark 10:45)

SCRIPTURE READINGS:

- Matthew 20:1-28
- Mark 10:31-45
- Luke 18:31-34

Questions? Learnings? Praises? Prayers? To Do's? Jesus is…?

DATE:

298 READING

JESUS' MINISTRY IN JERICHO — ZACCHAEUS, THE PARABLE OF THE TALENTS, AND HEALING THE BLIND

In Jericho, a wealthy tax collector promised to pay for what he stole, Jesus told him that salvation isn't what you do. It's a Person (Himself). Then Jesus told about a nobleman (Jesus) who gave riches (found in Jesus) to his ten servants (each Christian) to multiply (by making more disciples of Jesus) before He returned. Are you sharing the riches of Jesus with others?

> *And Jesus said to him, "Today salvation has come to this house, because he also is a son of Abraham; for the Son of Man has come to seek and to save that which was lost." (Luke 19:9–10)*

SCRIPTURE READINGS:

- Luke 19:1-27
- Matthew 25:14-30
- Mark 10:46-52

Questions? Learnings? Praises? Prayers? To Do's? Jesus is…?

DATE:

JESUS' TRIUMPHAL ENTRY — ENTERING JERUSALEM, CLEANSING THE TEMPLE, AND CURSING THE FIG TREE

Jesus entered Jerusalem exactly as Zechariah predicted. Israel's King of justice, salvation, and humility would enter the city on a donkey's colt. Jesus is the King. Is He your King? Are you finding justice, salvation, and humility in King Jesus? The crowds shouted for joy and cried out to Him, "Hosanna" ("Save us"). A few days later, the same crowds called for Him to be crucified.

299

READING

Rejoice greatly, O daughter of Zion! Shout, O daughter of Jerusalem! Behold, your King is coming to you; He is just and having salvation, Lowly and riding on a donkey, A colt, the foal of a donkey. (Zechariah 9:9)

SCRIPTURE READINGS:

- Matthew 21
- Psalms 118:19-29
- Zechariah 9:9

Questions? Learnings? Praises? Prayers? To Do's? Jesus is…?

DATE:

300 READING

JESUS' DEBATES WITH RELIGIOUS LEADERS — DEBATING THE PHARISEES, SADDUCEES, AND A LAWYER

The Jews asked Jesus about taxes (Did Jesus serve Caesar?), the kinsman redeemer law (Does Deuteronomy 25 prove there's no afterlife?), and the greatest commandment (It's love God. Do you love God more than anything?). Then Jesus asked His question. If the Messiah descended from David, why did David write as if the Messiah was alive? (He was. It was Jesus.)

> Jesus said to him, " 'You shall love the Lord your God with all your heart, with all your soul, and with all your mind.' This is the first and great commandment. (Matthew 22:37-38)

SCRIPTURE READINGS:

- Matthew 22
- Romans 13:1-7
- Psalms 110:1

Questions? Learnings? Praises? Prayers? To Do's? Jesus is...?

DATE:

301
REFLECTION AND PRAYER

Look Back at Last Week — List what God did and what God taught you over the last week. This is your "thank God list" for next week.

Look Forward to Next Week — List what events, decisions, deadlines, or progress needs to happen in the next week. This is your prayer list for next week.

DATE:

302 READING

JESUS' MESSAGE ON RELIGION — APPEARING RELIGIOUS VS. EXERCISING JUSTICE, MERCY, AND FAITH

Jesus the God-man revealed God's hatred of religious greed and hypocrisy. He whipped money changers out of the temple (Matthew 21). He preached against people who didn't practice what they preach, or prayed long to impress people, or did well while being watched. Has Jesus inside you given you His hatred of religious hypocrisy, especially when you see it in yourself?

But be doers of the word, and not hearers only, deceiving yourselves. (James 1:22)

SCRIPTURE READINGS:

- Matthew 23
- Micah 6:8
- James 1:22-27

Questions? Learnings? Praises? Prayers? To Do's? Jesus is…?

DATE:

JESUS' MINISTRY BEFORE HIS BETRAYAL — THE WIDOW'S MITE, END TIMES PROPHECY, AND GIVING

Financial giving wasn't confidential in Jesus' day. It was public knowledge. The disciples saw a widow give two inexpensive coins. Jesus said she gave more than the biggest donors because God sees the percentage. She gave 100% (like Jesus did). What percentage do you give? Then Jesus taught on two coming events: the destruction of the temple in 70 AD and the end times.

303 READING

> *So He called His disciples to Himself and said to them, "Assuredly, I say to you that this poor widow has put in more than all those who have given to the treasury; for they all put in out of their abundance, but she out of her poverty put in all that she had, her whole livelihood." (Mark 12:43–44)*

SCRIPTURE READINGS:

- Mark 12:38-44
- Luke 21
- 2 Corinthians 8:1-12

Questions? Learnings? Praises? Prayers? To Do's? Jesus is…?

DATE:

304 READING

JESUS' PASSOVER PREP — JUDAS' GREED AND BETRAYAL, MARY'S ANOINTING, AND THE FURNISHED ROOM

At a supper shortly before Jesus died, a woman anointed Him with a very expensive oil. Her gift was worth more than a year of salary but Jesus' fragrance filled the room. How much would you give to spread the fragrance and beauty of Jesus? The disciples criticized her. Judas wanted to steal it for himself. Jesus told them to leave her alone because she anointed Him for burial.

> *Assuredly, I say to you, wherever this gospel is preached in the whole world, what this woman has done will also be told as a memorial to her. (Matthew 26:13)*

SCRIPTURE READINGS:

- Matthew 26:1-19
- Luke 22:1-13
- John 12:4-6

Questions? Learnings? Praises? Prayers? To Do's? Jesus is...?

DATE:

JESUS' PASSOVER MEAL — JESUS CELEBRATES THE PASSOVER, PASSOVER'S ORIGIN, AND JUDAS LEAVES

Jesus celebrated Passover. It pictured Him. God delivered the Jews from slavery (salvation) when judgment "passed over" (forgiveness) any house with the lamb's blood (Jesus' cross). After Passover, Jesus showed shocking humility by washing the disciples' feet. Jesus will bless you if you do the same. Are you laying aside things in your life to serve His church with humility?

If I then, your Lord and Teacher, have washed your feet, you also ought to wash one another's feet. (John 13:14)

SCRIPTURE READINGS:

- Luke 22:14-18
- Exodus 12
- John 13:1-30

Questions? Learnings? Praises? Prayers? To Do's? Jesus is...?

DATE:

JESUS' PASSOVER INNOVATION — JESUS INSTITUTES COMMUNION (THE LORD'S SUPPER) FOR THE CHURCH

After celebrating the Jewish Passover, Jesus created Christian Communion (AKA the Lord's Supper). Communion pictures the cross: the bread, His broken body; the cup, His blood. Communion reminds you to examine yourself spiritually and confess any sins. Communion is a declaration that you're living in unity and mutual service with Jesus and His church. Are you?

> *For as often as you eat this bread and drink this cup, you proclaim the Lord's death till He comes. (1 Corinthians 11:26)*

SCRIPTURE READINGS:

- Luke 22:19-20
- 1 Corinthians 11:23-32
- 1 Corinthians 10:15-17

Questions? Learnings? Praises? Prayers? To Do's? Jesus is…?

DATE:

JESUS' PASSOVER TEACHINGS — JESUS SAYS HE LEAVES TO PREPARE A PLACE FOR HIS DISCIPLES

After Judas Iscariot left, Jesus taught the 11 what was about to happen. Jesus would depart (die) and be glorified with God in heaven. They couldn't come yet (die). He would prepare a home for them (in heaven). He would send the Holy Spirit to be His presence living inside them. Then He would return again. Are you living as if this world is your real home? Or the next?

307 READING

And if I go and prepare a place for you, I will come again and receive you to Myself; that where I am, there you may be also. (John 14:3)

SCRIPTURE READINGS:

- John 13:31-38
- John 14
- Hebrews 11:13-16

Questions? Learnings? Praises? Prayers? To Do's? Jesus is...?

DATE:

308
REFLECTION AND PRAYER

Look Back at Last Week — List what God did and what God taught you over the last week. This is your "thank God list" for next week.

Look Forward to Next Week — List what events, decisions, deadlines, or progress needs to happen in the next week. This is your prayer list for next week.

DATE:

JESUS' ARREST — JESUS' GARDEN PRAYER, KNOCKING THE MOB DOWN, HEALING AN EAR, AND ARREST

Jesus led the 11 to the Garden of Gethsemane in the dark. He asked Peter, James, and John to pray for Him. Do you ask friends to pray for you too? In agony, Jesus prayed for any other way but the cross. Jesus was fighting for our souls. When He found His three friends asleep, He asked, "Couldn't you pray one hour for Me?" This happened three times. Then Judas arrived.

READING

And He was withdrawn from them about a stone's throw, and He knelt down and prayed, 42 saying, "Father, if it is Your will, take this cup away from Me; nevertheless not My will, but Yours, be done." (Luke 22:41–42)

SCRIPTURE READINGS:

- Matthew 26:30-56
- Luke 22:39-53
- John 18:1-11

Questions? Learnings? Praises? Prayers? To Do's? Jesus is...?

DATE:

310 READING

JESUS' JEWISH TRIALS — JESUS' THREE JEWISH TRIALS AND PETER'S THREE DENIALS

After Jesus was arrested, He faced three Jewish trials. Annas questioned Him, Caiaphus found two liars to agree, and the council sentenced Him to death. Israel was murdering their Messiah. The apostles swore they'd never deny Jesus but Peter denied Him three times. Have you ever hidden that you follow Jesus? On the third time, Jesus looked at Peter who then fled and wept.

And Peter remembered the word of Jesus who had said to him, "Before the rooster crows, you will deny Me three times." So he went out and wept bitterly. (Matthew 26:75)

SCRIPTURE READINGS:

- John 18:12-27
- Matthew 26:57-75
- Luke 22:54-71

Questions? Learnings? Praises? Prayers? To Do's? Jesus is...?

DATE:

JESUS' ROMAN TRIALS — JESUS' THREE ROMAN TRIALS, RELEASING BARABBAS, AND JESUS' BEATINGS

After His three Jewish trials, Jesus faced three Roman trials. Pilate found Him innocent, Herod mocked Him, then Pilate scourged and beat and crucified Him. Have you reflected on the horrors Jesus suffered because He loves you? Barabbas pictured salvation. Barabbas was guilty of sin and deserved to die (like you). Barabbas was set free when Jesus took his place.

> *And he released to them the one they requested [Barabbas], who for rebellion and murder had been thrown into prison; but he delivered Jesus to their will. (Luke 23:25)*

SCRIPTURE READINGS:

- John 18:28-40
- Luke 23:1-25
- John 19:1-22

Questions? Learnings? Praises? Prayers? To Do's? Jesus is…?

DATE:

312 READING

JESUS' CRUCIFIXION — JESUS CARRIES THE CROSS, IS CRUCIFIED, AND JESUS' CALL TO CARRY YOUR CROSS

After He was sentenced to death, Jesus started carrying the cross (a cross beam up to 100 lbs). In exhaustion, Jesus fell. Simon carried the cross. His sons would know (Mark 15:21). Do others see you picking up the cross and following Jesus? Jesus was stripped naked, laid on the ground, and nailed to the cross. Jesus was fulfilling prophecies determined before time began.

Then they crucified Him, and divided His garments, casting lots, that it might be fulfilled which was spoken by the prophet: "They divided My garments among them, And for My clothing they cast lots." (Matthew 27:35)

SCRIPTURE READINGS:

- Matthew 27:31-44
- Acts 2:22-23
- Luke 14:25-33

Questions? Learnings? Praises? Prayers? To Do's? Jesus is…?

DATE:

JESUS' CONVERSATIONS — JESUS TALKS WITH WOMEN, SOLDIERS, AND THE THIEF ON THE CROSS

In His suffering, Jesus kept helping people. He urged weeping women to care for themselves. He asked God to forgive His enemies. He told John to care for His mom (John 19:26-27). He promised salvation to the thief who called him "Lord." Jesus showed us how to suffer. In your suffering, do you look for chances to minister for Jesus? Or are you only focused on yourself?

313

READING

And when they had come to the place called Calvary, there they crucified Him, and the criminals, one on the right hand and the other on the left. Then Jesus said, "Father, forgive them, for they do not know what they do." And they divided His garments and cast lots. (Luke 23:33–34)

SCRIPTURE READINGS:

- Luke 23:26-44
- 1 Corinthians 2:7-8
- 1 Peter 2:18-25

Questions? Learnings? Praises? Prayers? To Do's? Jesus is…?

DATE:

314 READING

JESUS' SUFFERING — VARIOUS PROPHECIES OF THE CROSS (MY GOD, I THIRST, GARMENTS DIVIDED, PIERCED)

Jesus was crucified at 9 a.m. At noon, God put every sin in history on Jesus then poured out His wrath against sin. Jesus suffered three hours of hell for us. In the dark, He cried, "I thirst" and "My God, My God, why have you forsaken Me?" Psalm 22 records Jesus' thoughts on the cross. Pause and express deep gratitude for His love and suffering. Pray that you and others love Him.

> *And at the ninth hour Jesus cried out with a loud voice, saying, "Eloi, Eloi, lama sabachthani?" which is translated, "My God, My God, why have You forsaken Me?" (Mark 15:34)*

SCRIPTURE READINGS:

- Mark 15:20-36
- John 19:23-37
- Psalms 22

Questions? Learnings? Praises? Prayers? To Do's? Jesus is…?

DATE:

315
REFLECTION AND PRAYER

Look Back at Last Week — List what God did and what God taught you over the last week. This is your "thank God list" for next week.

Look Forward to Next Week — List what events, decisions, deadlines, or progress needs to happen in the next week. This is your prayer list for next week.

DATE:

316 READING

JESUS' DEATH AND BURIAL — JESUS' DEATH ON THE CROSS AND BURIAL BY JOSEPH OF ARIMATHEA

Jesus cried with a loud voice and died at 3 p.m. Because of His grace, Jesus tasted death for you and destroyed the power of the devil. Has Jesus set you free from fearing death? When Jesus died, an earthquake hit, graves opened, the temple veil ripped, and the sun came out. This made the soldiers believe. Then Joseph buried Jesus and soldiers guarded His body.

Inasmuch then as the children have partaken of flesh and blood, He Himself likewise shared in the same, that through death He might destroy him who had the power of death, that is, the devil, (Hebrews 2:14)

SCRIPTURE READINGS:

- Matthew 27:45-66
- Luke 23:45-56
- Hebrews 2:9-18

Questions? Learnings? Praises? Prayers? To Do's? Jesus is...?

DATE:

JESUS' RESURRECTION — THE EMPTY TOMB, APPEARING TO MARY, AND ASCENDING TO HEAVEN

Early Sunday morning, women came to anoint Jesus' body but an angel said He was risen. The apostles saw the empty tomb but didn't believe He was risen. Then Jesus chose a woman He delivered from seven demons, Mary Magdalene, to be the first witness to His resurrection. Jesus didn't let Mary touch Him until He, as our High Priest, entered heaven with His blood.

317
READING

Then, as they were afraid and bowed their faces to the earth, they said to them, "Why do you seek the living among the dead? He is not here, but is risen! Remember how He spoke to you when He was still in Galilee, (Luke 24:5–6)

SCRIPTURE READINGS:

- Luke 24:1-12
- John 20:1-18
- Hebrews 9:16-28

Questions? Learnings? Praises? Prayers? To Do's? Jesus is...?

DATE:

318 READING

JESUS' RESURRECTION — JESUS APPEARS REPEATEDLY TO HIS UNBELIEVING DISCIPLES

Jesus proved He was alive by appearing 10 times over 40 days. His first five appearances were to Mary Magdalene, women, Peter, two disciples, and the apostles without Thomas. Jesus rebuked them for not believing He'd rise again and said, "Blessed are those that have not seen and have believed." Do you believe the people who saw Jesus and were changed forever?

Jesus said to him, "Thomas, because you have seen Me, you have believed. Blessed are those who have not seen and yet have believed." (John 20:29)

SCRIPTURE READINGS:

- Matthew 28
- Luke 24:13-53
- John 20:19-31

Questions? Learnings? Praises? Prayers? To Do's? Jesus is…?

DATE:

JESUS' RESURRECTION — JESUS PROVES HIS RESURRECTION OVER 40 DAYS

Jesus proved He was alive by appearing 10 times over 40 days. His second five appearances were to the apostles with Thomas, the seven at the Sea of Galilee, over 500, Jesus' half-brother James, and the apostles at His ascension. Why would you believe Jesus is alive? (1) The empty tomb. (2) The 10 appearances that changed people. (3) The spread of Christianity in a hostile environment.

319
READING

until the day in which He was taken up, after He through the Holy Spirit had given commandments to the apostles whom He had chosen, to whom He also presented Himself alive after His suffering by many infallible proofs, being seen by them during forty days and speaking of the things pertaining to the kingdom of God. (Acts 1:2–3)

SCRIPTURE READINGS:

- John 21
- Acts 1:1-4
- 1 Corinthians 15:1-19

Questions? Learnings? Praises? Prayers? To Do's? Jesus is...?

DATE:

320 READING

PETER — ASCENSION AND NEW APOSTLE — PROMISES ABOUT JESUS' RETURN AND PROPHECIES ABOUT JUDAS

Dr. Luke wrote Luke and Acts as a two-part story (Luke 1:1-4). Jesus told His disciples to wait for the Spirit in Jerusalem then take the gospel to their city, region, and world. Are you helping take the gospel to your city, region, and world? Then Jesus ascended from where He will return (Zechariah 14). When Peter realized Psalm 109 said to replace Judas, Matthias replaced him.

> *But you shall receive power when the Holy Spirit has come upon you; and you shall be witnesses to Me [Jesus] in Jerusalem, and in all Judea and Samaria, and to the end of the earth." (Acts 1:8)*

SCRIPTURE READINGS:

- Acts 1
- Luke 21:25-28
- Psalms 109

Questions? Learnings? Praises? Prayers? To Do's? Jesus is…?

DATE:

PETER — PENTECOST — THE MIRACLE OF TONGUES AND THE PURPOSE OF TONGUES (FOR UNBELIEVERS)

When Jesus sent the Holy Spirit at Pentecost, Jews from 15 regions heard Galileans speak their languages. God used this publicly as a sign to the unbelievers. Peter preached Joel 2, called people to Jesus, and baptized 3,000. The new believers engaged daily with each other in the church. Read Acts 2:42-47 and listen to the Holy Spirit about your engagement with the church.

321

READING

Then those who gladly received his word were baptized; and that day about three thousand souls were added to them. (Acts 2:41)

SCRIPTURE READINGS:

- Acts 2
- Joel 2:28-32
- 1 Corinthians 14:18-25

Questions? Learnings? Praises? Prayers? To Do's? Jesus is…?

DATE:

322
REFLECTION AND PRAYER

Look Back at Last Week — List what God did and what God taught you over the last week. This is your "thank God list" for next week.

Look Forward to Next Week — List what events, decisions, deadlines, or progress needs to happen in the next week. This is your prayer list for next week.

DATE:

PETER — THE LAME MAN HEALED AND APOSTLES ARRESTED — PETER AND JOHN'S BOLD MESSAGE

Peter and John healed a lame man by the temple in Jesus' name. Peter preached to the crowds that gathered and the church grew to 5,000. Peter and John were arrested. Peter was filled with the Spirit and preached Jesus boldly to them. After Peter and John were released, the church prayed for boldness. Pray now for yourself and your church to share Jesus with boldness.

323 READING

And when they had prayed, the place where they were assembled together was shaken; and they were all filled with the Holy Spirit, and they spoke the word of God with boldness. (Acts 4:31)

SCRIPTURE READINGS:

- Acts 3
- Acts 4
- Ephesians 6:18-20

Questions? Learnings? Praises? Prayers? To Do's? Jesus is...?

DATE:

324 READING

PETER — REARRESTED, TRIED, AND BEATEN FOR PREACHING — THE HONOR OF SUFFERING FOR JESUS

Ananias and Saphira lied to Jesus and the church about their giving and God took them home. Then Peter and John were arrested again for preaching Jesus. Peter said, "We ought to obey God rather than men." Then Peter and John rejoiced in being beaten for Jesus. Jesus said you are blessed when you're criticized or persecuted for Him. Do you rejoice in suffering for Jesus?

> *And they agreed with him, and when they had called for the apostles and beaten them, they commanded that they should not speak in the name of Jesus, and let them go. So they departed from the presence of the council, rejoicing that they were counted worthy to suffer shame for His name. (Acts 5:40–41)*

SCRIPTURE READINGS:

- Acts 5
- Matthew 5:10-12
- 1 Peter 3:13-17

Questions? Learnings? Praises? Prayers? To Do's? Jesus is...?

DATE:

PETER — THE FIRST DEACONS — THE DEACON'S MINISTRY FREES UP ELDERS TO FOCUS ON THE WORD

The church grew so fast that their support systems broke. Greek-speaking widows didn't receive care. When you hear of problems, do you ignore, dispute, or ask Jesus how to address it? The church identified seven men with Christ's character, the Holy Spirit, and wisdom to serve (or "deacon"). When the apostles focused on prayer and the word, Jesus grew the church more.

Then the word of God spread, and the number of the disciples multiplied greatly in Jerusalem, and a great many of the priests were obedient to the faith. (Acts 6:7)

SCRIPTURE READINGS:

- Acts 6
- 1 Timothy 5:17-18
- 1 Timothy 3:8-13

Questions? Learnings? Praises? Prayers? To Do's? Jesus is...?

DATE:

326 READING

PETER — STEPHEN'S MESSAGE AND MARTYRDOM — LOOKING TO JESUS AND FORGIVING WRONGDOERS

Stephen performed miracles and preached (like Jesus). The Jews lied and arrested Stephen (like Jesus). Stephen preached Israel's history, concluding they murdered their Messiah. Stephen prayed for his murderers (like Jesus). As Stephen died, he was looking to Jesus. Looking to Jesus helps you run the race God has for you. What does it mean to look to Jesus?

> *looking unto Jesus, the author and finisher of our faith, who for the joy that was set before Him endured the cross, despising the shame, and has sat down at the right hand of the throne of God. For consider Him who endured such hostility from sinners against Himself, lest you become weary and discouraged in your souls. (Hebrews 12:2-3)*

SCRIPTURE READINGS:

- Acts 7
- Hebrews 12:1-3
- Luke 23:32-34

Questions? Learnings? Praises? Prayers? To Do's? Jesus is...?

DATE:

PETER — ETHIOPIAN EUNUCH — DISCUSSING ISAIAH 53, A 700-YEAR OLD PROPHECY ABOUT JESUS

When Phillip preached Jesus in Samaria (a city Jews avoided), revival began. God told Philip to leave the revival without saying why. Do you love Jesus enough to obey when you don't see why? Philip explained Isaiah 53 to the treasurer of the Ethiopian queen. The prophecy was about Jesus. The man was baptized and returned to Ethiopia as an influential new Christian.

327 READING

Then Philip opened his mouth, and beginning at this Scripture, preached Jesus to him. (Acts 8:35)

SCRIPTURE READINGS:

- Acts 8:4-40
- Isaiah 53
- Acts 9:32-43

Questions? Learnings? Praises? Prayers? To Do's? Jesus is...?

DATE:

328 READING

PETER — CORNELIUS' CONVERSION — GOD BRINGS GENTILES (NON-JEWS) INTO GOD'S HOUSEHOLD

Cornelius was a Roman centurion who supported the Jews, prayed all the time, and gave to the poor. Jews avoided him because he was a Gentile. God gave visions to Cornelius and Peter to bring them together. As Peter preached in Cornelius' house, God interrupted him by giving the Gentiles the Holy Spirit. Did you know that racial reconciliation is embedded in the Gospel?

> *When they heard these things they became silent; and they glorified God, saying, "Then God has also granted to the Gentiles repentance to life." (Acts 11:18)*

SCRIPTURE READINGS:

- Acts 10
- Acts 11:1-18
- Ephesians 2:11-22

Questions? Learnings? Praises? Prayers? To Do's? Jesus is...?

DATE:

329
REFLECTION AND PRAYER

Look Back at Last Week — List what God did and what God taught you over the last week. This is your "thank God list" for next week.

Look Forward to Next Week — List what events, decisions, deadlines, or progress needs to happen in the next week. This is your prayer list for next week.

DATE:

PETER — JERUSALEM PERSECUTION — DO NOT GIVE UP ON PRAYER NOR DOUBT THAT GOD ANSWERS PRAYER

Herod killed James the apostle then arrested Peter. The church gathered to pray for him. When God set Peter free, he came to the door. Rhoda told those praying that Peter was there. They didn't believe her. Do you believe God when you pray? Jesus told a parable about not giving up in prayer. Is the Holy Spirit prompting you to start praying again for something you stopped?

Then He spoke a parable to them, that men always ought to pray and not lose heart, (Luke 18:1)

SCRIPTURE READINGS:

- Acts 12:1-24
- Luke 18:1-8
- James 1:2-8

Questions? Learnings? Praises? Prayers? To Do's? Jesus is...?

DATE:

PAUL — SALVATION — SAUL (LATER KNOWN AS "PAUL") PERSECUTES THE CHURCH AND MEETS JESUS

Paul was originally Saul, a zealous Jewish leader who arrested and murdered the church. Jesus appeared to him on his way to Damascus to arrest Christians. Blinded by the light, he fell and heard he persecuted Jesus. After three days in shock, he was baptized and preached Jesus. Saul's conversion is another proof of Christianity and hope that Jesus can reach anyone.

331

READING

And he said, "Who are You, Lord?" Then the Lord said, "I am Jesus, whom you are persecuting. It is hard for you to kick against the goads." So he, trembling and astonished, said, "Lord, what do You want me to do?" Then the Lord said to him, "Arise and go into the city, and you will be told what you must do." (Acts 9:5–6)

SCRIPTURE READINGS:

- Acts 8:1-3
- Acts 9:1-31
- Galatians 1:10-24

Questions? Learnings? Praises? Prayers? To Do's? Jesus is…?

DATE:

332 READING

PAUL — ANTIOCH — A NEW CHURCH PLANT, SENDING RELIEF TO JERUSALEM, AND BEING GOOD STEWARDS

The church in Jerusalem had to be persecuted to take the Gospel elsewhere. When Christian refugees arrived in Antioch, God brought many Gentiles to Jesus. Barnabas and Saul discipled them for a year. Jesus moved the church in Antioch to give to the church in Jerusalem. Jesus gave you everything you have. Are you managing Jesus' resources in ways that glorify Him?

> *And when he had found him, he brought him to Antioch. So it was that for a whole year they assembled with the church and taught a great many people. And the disciples were first called Christians in Antioch. (Acts 11:26)*

SCRIPTURE READINGS:

- Acts 11:19-30
- Acts 12:25
- 1 Peter 4:7-11

Questions? Learnings? Praises? Prayers? To Do's? Jesus is…?

DATE:

PAUL — JOURNEY #1 (CYPRUS, ANTIOCH OF PISIDIA) — THE CHURCH AT ANTIOCH SENDS MISSIONARIES

The church in Antioch wasn't forced to take the gospel to the world. As they worshiped, the Holy Spirit led them to send Barnabas and Saul. Are you led by the Holy Spirit? Are you helping reach people around the world? This was Paul's first missionary journey. Paul's strategy was to find the synagogue in a city, preach Jesus, and organize the new converts into a new church.

333 READING

> *As they ministered to the Lord and fasted, the Holy Spirit said, "Now separate to Me Barnabas and Saul for the work to which I have called them." (Acts 13:2)*

SCRIPTURE READINGS:

- Acts 13
- Matthew 28:18-20
- Acts 1:8

Questions? Learnings? Praises? Prayers? To Do's? Jesus is...?

DATE:

334 READING

PAUL — JOURNEY #1 (ICONIUM, LYSTRA, DERBE) — PAUL'S MIRACLES, MESSAGE, AND SUFFERING

Paul desired to preach to people who never heard of Jesus. That's also Jesus' desire. Paul and Barnabas were persecuted in Antioch in Pisidia (expelled), Iconium (threatened), and Lystra (Paul was stoned and left for dead). Paul wrote that all who want to live godly in Christ Jesus will suffer. When you love someone, you'll suffer for them. Jesus loved you. Do you love Jesus?

Yes, and all who desire to live godly in Christ Jesus will suffer persecution. (2 Timothy 3:12)

SCRIPTURE READINGS:

- Acts 14
- 2 Timothy 3:10-13
- Romans 15:15-21

Questions? Learnings? Praises? Prayers? To Do's? Jesus is...?

DATE:

PAUL — CHURCH COUNCIL AT JERUSALEM — THE OLD TESTAMENT LAWS, CIRCUMCISION, AND THE GENTILES

The early church debated if Gentiles could become Christians without becoming Jews (i.e. circumcision, Sabbath rest, no pork, etc.). A church council determined that Gentiles were free from Moses' law but should avoid idolatry and sexual immorality. Jesus sets people free from the Law to live for Him. Like Paul, can you say, "It is no longer I who live, but Christ lives in me"?

335 READING

I have been crucified with Christ; it is no longer I who live, but Christ lives in me; and the life which I now live in the flesh I live by faith in the Son of God, who loved me and gave Himself for me. I do not set aside the grace of God; for if righteousness comes through the law, then Christ died in vain." (Galatians 2:20–21)

SCRIPTURE READINGS:

- Acts 15:1-35
- Acts 21:25
- Galatians 2

Questions? Learnings? Praises? Prayers? To Do's? Jesus is...?

DATE:

336

REFLECTION AND PRAYER

Look Back at Last Week — List what God did and what God taught you over the last week. This is your "thank God list" for next week.

Look Forward to Next Week — List what events, decisions, deadlines, or progress needs to happen in the next week. This is your prayer list for next week.

DATE:

PAUL — JOURNEY #2 (PAUL AND BARNABAS SPLIT UP) — JOHN MARK QUITS AND LEARNS NOT TO QUIT

John Mark showed that Jesus is a God of second chances. His cousin Barnabas brought him to Antioch but he quit Paul's first missionary journey (Acts 12-13). To Paul, he was a quitter. Paul and Barnabas split over whether to give him a second chance. Later he served with Peter and wrote the Gospel of Mark. Do you give yourself and others the second chances of Jesus?

Aristarchus my fellow prisoner greets you, with Mark the cousin of Barnabas (about whom you received instructions: if he comes to you, welcome him), and Jesus who is called Justus. These are my only fellow workers for the kingdom of God who are of the circumcision; they have proved to be a comfort to me. (Colossians 4:10–11)

SCRIPTURE READINGS:

- Acts 15:36-41
- Colossians 4:10-11
- 2 Timothy 4:9-18

Questions? Learnings? Praises? Prayers? To Do's? Jesus is…?

DATE:

338 READING

PAUL — JOURNEY #2 (DERBE) — THE STORY OF PAUL AND TIMOTHY (AS SPIRITUAL PARENT AND CHILD)

Timothy showed how families and the church work together to make four generations of disciples (2 Timothy 2:2). Timothy's family helped him believe in Jesus and begin serving. What is your family helping kids do? Then Paul became his spiritual father when he took him on his second journey. Are you helping people in the church love Jesus and spread the Gospel?

> *when I [Paul] call to remembrance the genuine faith that is in you [Timothy], which dwelt first in your grandmother Lois and your mother Eunice, and I am persuaded is in you also. (2 Timothy 1:5)*

SCRIPTURE READINGS:

- Acts 16:1-5
- 2 Timothy 1:1-14
- Philippians 2:19-24

Questions? Learnings? Praises? Prayers? To Do's? Jesus is...?

DATE:

PAUL — JOURNEY #2 (LYSTRA, PHILIPPI) — PAUL'S SUFFERING AT PHILIPPI AND OTHER PLACES

The Holy Spirit told Paul no to one direction and blocked another. Has Jesus told you no to guide you? Paul saw a vision of a man from Macedonia and preached to a group of women. Paul and Silas were beaten severely. In jail, they sang to God. An earthquake opened the jail. The jailer's whole house received Jesus. Paul suffered greatly because Jesus used him greatly.

339

READING

> ...they were forbidden by the Holy Spirit to preach the word in Asia... they tried to go into Bithynia, but the Spirit did not permit them... And a vision appeared to Paul in the night. A man of Macedonia stood and pleaded with him, saying, "Come over to Macedonia and help us." (Acts 16:6-7, 9)

SCRIPTURE READINGS:

- Acts 16:6-40
- 1 Thessalonians 2:1-12
- 2 Corinthians 11:22-33

Questions? Learnings? Praises? Prayers? To Do's? Jesus is...?

DATE:

TIM HOWEY | 345

340 READING

PAUL — JOURNEY #2 (THESSALONICA, BEREA, ATHENS) — PAUL'S MINISTRY TO THESSALONICA

Paul planted a church in Thessalonica but had to flee. Concerned, he sent Timothy back. Later he sent the letter of 1 Thessalonians. Paul called his disciples his "hope, joy, crown of rejoicing, and glory." Aside from Jesus, are your disciples your greatest treasures in the world? At Athens, Paul used an altar "To The Unknown God" to preach, "He's not unknown to me. He's Jesus."

For what is our hope, or joy, or crown of rejoicing? Is it not even you [the church in Thessalonica] in the presence of our Lord Jesus Christ at His coming? (1 Thessalonians 2:19)

SCRIPTURE READINGS:

- Acts 17
- 1 Thessalonians 2:13-20
- 1 Thessalonians 3

Questions? Learnings? Praises? Prayers? To Do's? Jesus is...?

DATE:

PAUL — JOURNEY #2 (CORINTH, EPHESUS, ANTIOCH) — THE STORY OF AQUILA AND PRISCILLA

Priscilla and Aquila served Jesus together throughout their marriage. In Rome, they were expelled for being Jews. In Corinth, they started a tent business with Paul and helped him plant a church. They joined Paul's journey and risked their lives with him for Jesus. Together, they led Apollos to Christ. If you're married, are you helping each other love Jesus and serve Him?

341 READING

Greet Priscilla and Aquila, my fellow workers in Christ Jesus, who risked their own necks for my life, to whom not only I give thanks, but also all the churches of the Gentiles. (Romans 16:3–4)

SCRIPTURE READINGS:

- Acts 18
- 1 Corinthians 16:19
- Romans 16:3-5

Questions? Learnings? Praises? Prayers? To Do's? Jesus is…?

DATE:

342 READING

PAUL — JOURNEY #3 (APOLLOS) — THE STORIES OF PAUL AND APOLLOS (AS CO-LABORERS)

Like John the Baptist, Apollos was preaching to prepare people for the Messiah. When Aquila and Priscilla told him the Messiah came, he preached Jesus. At Corinth, he helped the church grow greatly. Immature Christians began arguing over which minister was more important. Have you fallen into the trap of the celebrity minister? A minister is only an instrument of God.

Who then is Paul, and who is Apollos, but ministers through whom you believed, as the Lord gave to each one? (1 Corinthians 3:5)

SCRIPTURE READINGS:

- Acts 18:24-28
- 1 Corinthians 1:10-17
- 1 Corinthians 3:1-8

Questions? Learnings? Praises? Prayers? To Do's? Jesus is...?

DATE:

343

REFLECTION AND PRAYER

Look Back at Last Week — List what God did and what God taught you over the last week. This is your "thank God list" for next week.

Look Forward to Next Week — List what events, decisions, deadlines, or progress needs to happen in the next week. This is your prayer list for next week.

DATE:

344 READING

PAUL — JOURNEY #3 (EPHESUS) — THE STORY OF THE CHURCH AT EPHESUS THROUGH SCRIPTURE

In Ephesus, Paul planted a church with converts from the synagogue then preached to Gentiles in a school. The church shared Jesus throughout the region. Ephesians and 1 Timothy showed the church at Ephesus was healthy. A generation later, Revelation revealed that the church was so busy they left their first love (Jesus). Are you so busy that you left your first love (Jesus)?

Nevertheless I have this against you, that you have left your first love. (Revelation 2:4)

SCRIPTURE READINGS:

- Acts 19
- 1 Timothy 1:1-7
- Revelation 2:1-7

Questions? Learnings? Praises? Prayers? To Do's? Jesus is...?

DATE:

PAUL — JOURNEY #3 (PLAN FOR ROME) — PAUL'S PLAN TO VISIT ROME AFTER VISITING JERUSALEM

In Ephesus, Paul planned a mission trip to Rome. When he wrote Romans, he shared his plan. Paul had not been to Rome but he heard about them, prayed for them, and wanted to travel there to grow one another spiritually. Has Jesus grown a deep care in you for churches around the world? Pause and pray for churches around the world. Ask God if you should join a trip.

> *For I long to see you, that I may impart to you some spiritual gift, so that you may be established—that is, that I may be encouraged together with you by the mutual faith both of you and me. (Romans 1:11–12)*

SCRIPTURE READINGS:

- Acts 19:20-22
- Romans 1:8-17
- Romans 15:20-33

Questions? Learnings? Praises? Prayers? To Do's? Jesus is…?

DATE:

346 READING

PAUL — JOURNEY #3 (MACEDONIA, TROAS) — PAUL TEACHES THE ELDERS HOW TO SHEPHERD

Paul called the Ephesian elders (AKA bishops/overseers, pastors/shepherds) to a retreat. He prepared them for external and internal attacks their church would face. Then he shared how Jesus protects His church. "I commend you [church leaders] to God and to the word of His grace which is able." Are you living in the spiritual protection of church leaders, God, and the BIble?

So now, brethren, I commend you to God and to the word of His grace, which is able to build you up and give you an inheritance among all those who are sanctified. (Acts 20:32)

SCRIPTURE READINGS:

- Acts 20
- Titus 1:5-10
- 1 Peter 5:1-11

Questions? Learnings? Praises? Prayers? To Do's? Jesus is...?

DATE:

PAUL — ARREST IN JERUSALEM — THE JEWS OPPOSE PAUL FOR BEING CALLED TO THE GENTILES

Paul purposed in the Spirit to head to Jerusalem (Acts 19:21). In Tyre, disciples said through the Spirit to stop (Acts 21:4). Paul went anyway. Are you open to Jesus speaking through others? When the Jews attacked Paul thinking he brought Gentiles into the temple, soldiers saved him. Paul told the crowd how he met Jesus. Ask God who you should tell how you met Jesus. Listen.

And finding disciples, we stayed there seven days. They told Paul through the Spirit not to go up to Jerusalem. (Acts 21:4)

SCRIPTURE READINGS:

- Acts 21
- Acts 22
- Philippians 3

Questions? Learnings? Praises? Prayers? To Do's? Jesus is...?

DATE:

348 READING

PAUL — JOURNEY #4 (JERUSALEM, CAESAREA) — THE SADDUCEES, PHARISEES, AND PAUL'S TRIAL BEFORE FELIX

The Roman commander summoned the Jewish council to see why Paul was attacked. A fight ended the meeting. That night, Jesus told Paul he would preach in Rome someday. Paul was taken to Caesarea where he shared Jesus with the Roman governor Felix. For two years, Paul waited and ministered. Did you know suffering for Jesus is as much a gift as your faith in Him?

For to you it has been granted on behalf of Christ, not only to believe in Him, but also to suffer for His sake, (Philippians 1:29)

SCRIPTURE READINGS:

- Acts 23
- Acts 24
- Philippians 1:27-30

Questions? Learnings? Praises? Prayers? To Do's? Jesus is…?

DATE:

PAUL — JOURNEY #4 (CAESAREA) — PAUL'S TRIALS AND SUBMITTING TO THE LAWS OF THE GOVERNMENT

After two years, Paul stood before the new Roman governor Festus. Paul said he obeyed every Roman law and was willing to die if he deserved it. Then he officially appealed his case to Caesar. Jesus' followers obey laws, even when they disagree, until they are forced to disobey God. When you speak, do people hear Jesus honoring political leaders you don't agree with?

349 READING

Therefore submit yourselves to every ordinance of man for the Lord's sake, whether to the king as supreme... For this is the will of God, that by doing good you may put to silence the ignorance of foolish men— (1 Peter 2:13, 15)

SCRIPTURE READINGS:

- Acts 25
- Acts 26
- 1 Peter 2:11-17

Questions? Learnings? Praises? Prayers? To Do's? Jesus is...?

DATE:

350
REFLECTION AND PRAYER

Look Back at Last Week — List what God did and what God taught you over the last week. This is your "thank God list" for next week.

Look Forward to Next Week — List what events, decisions, deadlines, or progress needs to happen in the next week. This is your prayer list for next week.

DATE:

PAUL — JOURNEY #4 (SHIPWRECK, MALTA, ROME) — ONESIPHORUS CARES FOR PAUL IN PRISON

When Paul thought his ship would sink and people would die, God promised to save the people. In Rome, Paul preached Jesus to the Jewish leaders. Some Christians were ashamed of Paul in jail. Onesiphorus often visited Paul in jail. Jesus talked of visiting people in jail too (Matthew 25). Ask God's Spirit to help you remember Christians in prison as if you're with them (Hebrews 13).

351
READING

So when they had appointed him a day, many came to him at his lodging, to whom he explained and solemnly testified of the kingdom of God, persuading them concerning Jesus from both the Law of Moses and the Prophets, from morning till evening. (Acts 28:23)

SCRIPTURE READINGS:

- Acts 27
- Acts 28
- 2 Timothy 1:15-18

Questions? Learnings? Praises? Prayers? To Do's? Jesus is...?

DATE:

352 READING

PETER AND PAUL — PETER AND PAUL FINISH THEIR LIFE WELL AND ARE PREPARED FOR ETERNITY

In Peter's final letter, he wrote how to follow Jesus so people would follow Him after he was gone. In Paul's final letter, he wrote that he wanted to finish his race well. Jesus changes how His followers view life and death. To Paul, death was far better than life yet he knew he was alive to minister for Jesus. Has the Holy Spirit changed you to view life and death this way too?

> *For I am hard-pressed between the two, having a desire to depart and be with Christ, which is far better. Nevertheless to remain in the flesh is more needful for you. (Philippians 1:23–24)*

SCRIPTURE READINGS:

- 2 Peter 1:1-15
- Philippians 1:12-26
- 2 Timothy 4:1-8

Questions? Learnings? Praises? Prayers? To Do's? Jesus is…?

DATE:

REVELATION AND THE END TIMES — JESUS' SOON RETURN WILL MARK THE END OF A "SPIRITUAL NIGHT"

When Jesus was in the world, it was "spiritual day." He was "the light of the world" (John 9). When Jesus left, the world entered "spiritual night." Today Jesus' followers are like the moon, reflecting the light of Jesus (Matthew 5). Do people see Jesus shining through you in this world? Are you spiritually awake or asleep? When Jesus returns, "spiritual day" will dawn once again.

353

READING

The night is far spent, the day is at hand. Therefore let us cast off the works of darkness, and let us put on the armor of light. (Romans 13:12)

SCRIPTURE READINGS:

- Revelation 1
- 1 Thessalonians 5:1-11
- Romans 13:8-14

Questions? Learnings? Praises? Prayers? To Do's? Jesus is…?

DATE:

354 READING

REVELATION AND THE SEVEN CHURCHES — JESUS' PROMISE TO THE CHURCH WILL BE FULFILLED BY HIM

In Revelation, Jesus sent seven messages to seven churches. For each church, Jesus revealed who He is, what was going well, what was not going well, and how to return to Him. Jesus didn't mention how big the churches were. Success isn't related to a church's size. It's related to their love and faithfulness to Him. Are you committed to a church that loves Jesus and follows Him?

> *And I also say to you that you are Peter, and on this rock I will build My church, and the gates of Hades shall not prevail against it. (Matthew 16:18)*

SCRIPTURE READINGS:

- Revelation 2
- Revelation 3
- Matthew 16:18

Questions? Learnings? Praises? Prayers? To Do's? Jesus is…?

DATE:

REVELATION AND THE TRUMPET — PEOPLE WILL BE CALLED SUDDENLY INTO GOD'S PRESENCE

John heard a voice like a trumpet saying, "Come up." Instantly he was in God's presence and all worshiped Jesus. One day, Jesus will catch away His church. A trumpet will sound, the bodies of dead believers will rise, then living believers will be caught into His presence. Are you struggling to remain steadfast to the Lord or hopeful in death? Fix your mind on Jesus' return.

355 READING

> *Then we who are alive and remain shall be caught up together with them in the clouds to meet the Lord in the air. And thus we shall always be with the Lord. Therefore comfort one another with these words. (1 Thessalonians 4:17–18)*

SCRIPTURE READINGS:

- Revelation 4
- 1 Corinthians 15:35-58
- 1 Thessalonians 4:13-18

Questions? Learnings? Praises? Prayers? To Do's? Jesus is…?

DATE:

356 READING

REVELATION AND THE TRIBULATION — GOD'S JUDGMENT WILL BE POURED ON THE WORLD

Jesus said the world will face great tribulation someday. After wars, false prophets, signs, and mourning, Jesus will return. John saw a dragon (Satan), a miraculously-healed beast (antichrist) and a beast speaking like the dragon (false prophet). John saw people not turning back to God in spite of God's wrath poured out on sins. Jesus said to watch for His return. Are you watching?

Watch therefore, for you do not know what hour your Lord is coming. (Matthew 24:42)

SCRIPTURE READINGS:

- Revelation 13
- Revelation 16
- Matthew 24

Questions? Learnings? Praises? Prayers? To Do's? Jesus is…?

DATE:

357

REFLECTION AND PRAYER

Look Back at Last Week — List what God did and what God taught you over the last week. This is your "thank God list" for next week.

Look Forward to Next Week — List what events, decisions, deadlines, or progress needs to happen in the next week. This is your prayer list for next week.

DATE:

358 READING

REVELATION AND THE MARRIAGE SUPPER — JESUS CHRIST WILL MARRY HIS BRIDE, THE CHURCH

Jesus created husbands and wives to picture Himself and His bride the church (Ephesians 5). If you received Jesus, you're not married yet. You're engaged. You accepted Jesus' proposal. Are you as faithful to Jesus as a loving fiancée? Are you fully devoted to Jesus and the gospel? One day, Jesus will marry His church and host a feast called the marriage supper of the Lamb.

For I am jealous for you with godly jealousy. For I have betrothed you to one husband, that I may present you as a chaste virgin to Christ. But I fear, lest somehow, as the serpent deceived Eve by his craftiness, so your minds may be corrupted from the simplicity that is in Christ. (2 Corinthians 11:2–3)

SCRIPTURE READINGS:

- Revelation 19:1-10
- Matthew 22:1-14
- 2 Corinthians 11:1-4

Questions? Learnings? Praises? Prayers? To Do's? Jesus is...?

DATE:

REVELATION AND THE SECOND COMING — CHRIST WILL RETURN TO THE EARTH IN POWER AND GLORY

The greatest days for humanity were Jesus' death and resurrection. The day mentioned most in Scripture is Jesus' second coming (AKA "the day of the Lord, day of God, that day"). Jesus will come in power and great glory to defeat His enemies, save His people, and establish His throne on earth. Is Jesus fulfilling His good pleasure in you so His name will be glorified on that day?

359 READING

> *Now I saw heaven opened, and behold, a white horse. And He who sat on him was called Faithful and True, and in righteousness He judges and makes war... And He has on His robe and on His thigh a name written: KING OF KINGS AND LORD OF LORDS (Revelation 19:11, 16)*

SCRIPTURE READINGS:

- Revelation 19:11-21
- Zechariah 14:1-15
- 2 Thessalonians 1

Questions? Learnings? Praises? Prayers? To Do's? Jesus is...?

DATE:

360 READING

REVELATION AND THE MILLENNIUM — JESUS CHRIST WILL REIGN ON EARTH AFTER HIS RETURN

Zechariah had a vision of Jesus touching down on the Mount of Olives, becoming King over all the earth, and having nations worship Him in Jerusalem. John had a vision of Jesus locking Satan up and reigning with His people for 1000 years. Jesus told a parable about letting His faithful servants reign with Him. In Jesus' parable in Luke 19, which character are you?

> *And so it was that when he returned, having received the kingdom, he then commanded these servants, to whom he had given the money, to be called to him, that he might know how much every man had gained by trading... And he said to him, 'Well done, good servant; because you were faithful in a very little, have authority over ten cities.' (Luke 19:15, 17)*

SCRIPTURE READINGS:

- Revelation 20:1-10
- Zechariah 14:16-21
- Luke 19:11-27

Questions? Learnings? Praises? Prayers? To Do's? Jesus is...?

DATE:

REVELATION AND THE FINAL JUDGMENT — GOD WILL JUDGE PEOPLE BY THE PERFECT STANDARD OF JESUS

At the great white throne judgment, people without Jesus face terrifying fairness. Every thought, word, and action are judged against the perfect standard of Christ. Jesus came because it was impossible for us to survive God's justice. God judges a Christian's service for Him instead of sins which Jesus paid (1 Corinthians 3). Do you live as if you believe the final judgment is real?

in the day when God will judge the secrets of men by Jesus Christ, according to my gospel. (Romans 2:16)

SCRIPTURE READINGS:

- Revelation 20:11-13
- Romans 2:1-16
- Romans 3:9-26

Questions? Learnings? Praises? Prayers? To Do's? Jesus is...?

DATE:

362 READING

REVELATION AND THE FINAL CONSEQUENCES — SOME WILL EXPERIENCE THE SECOND, ETERNAL DEATH

When God's people died in the Old Testament, they rested in paradise. At His ascension, Jesus moved paradise and God's people to heaven. Now when Christians die, they go to heaven. When people without God die, they go to hell to wait for judgment and the lake of fire. Are you sharing the realities of two futures: God's eternal judgment for sins or eternal life with Christ?

> *So it was that the beggar died, and was carried by the angels to Abraham's bosom. The rich man also died and was buried. And being in torments in Hades, he lifted up his eyes and saw Abraham afar off, and Lazarus in his bosom. (Luke 16:22–23)*

SCRIPTURE READINGS:

- Revelation 20:14-15
- Luke 16:19-31
- Isaiah 66:22-24

Questions? Learnings? Praises? Prayers? To Do's? Jesus is…?

DATE:

REVELATION AND THE RENOVATED UNIVERSE — THERE WILL BE A NEW HEAVEN, EARTH, AND JERUSALEM

After the final judgment, Jesus will dissolve the old heavens and old earth with a great noise and fire. After that, no one will think of this world. How much time do you spend investing in things that will be forgotten forever? Then Jesus will make a new heaven and a new earth where there are no more tears, death, sorrow, pain, or sin. In its place is Jesus' life, love, joy, and glory.

363 READING

> *Nevertheless we, according to His promise, look for new heavens and a new earth in which righteousness dwells. (2 Peter 3:13)*

SCRIPTURE READINGS:

- Revelation 21
- Isaiah 65:17-25
- 2 Peter 3

Questions? Learnings? Praises? Prayers? To Do's? Jesus is…?

DATE:

364
REFLECTION AND PRAYER

Look Back at Last Week — List what God did and what God taught you over the last week. This is your "thank God list" for next week.

Look Forward to Next Week — List what events, decisions, deadlines, or progress needs to happen in the next week. This is your prayer list for next week.

DATE:

REVELATION AND ETERNITY FUTURE — JESUS CHRIST'S KINGDOM WILL LAST FOREVER AND EVER AND EVER AND EVER...

At the start, God and His people loved each other by a tree of life. Sin caused a detour. At the end, we're back at the start. Everyone chosen in Christ will be gathered together, loved, and made acceptable because of Jesus. The increase of Jesus' government and peace will never end. Do you know Jesus created the universe and you to share His love, joy, and purposes?

365 READING

> *just as He chose us in Him before the foundation of the world, that we should be holy and without blame before Him in love... that in the dispensation of the fullness of the times He might gather together in one all things in Christ, both which are in heaven and which are on earth—in Him. (Ephesians 1:4, 10)*

SCRIPTURE READINGS:

- Revelation 22
- Isaiah 9:6-7
- Ephesians 1:1-14

Questions? Learnings? Praises? Prayers? To Do's? Jesus is...?

DATE:

WHAT'S NEXT?

What's next is that you continue to grow in the belief and security of knowing Jesus loves you completely and unconditionally.

What's next is that you continue to grow in your love for Jesus, your enjoyment of Him, and your deep sense of contentment that Jesus is enough for you.

What's next is that you continue to cultivate a lifestyle of connecting with Jesus through reading the Bible, praying to Him, and listening to His Holy Spirit.

What's next is that you help someone else to do the same, passing on what you've learned to a second generation spiritually, who passes it on to a third generation spiritually, who passes it on to a fourth generation spiritually.

I'll see you and Jesus soon (Revelation 22:21).

With love,
Tim

BIO

Tim is the founding and senior pastor of Grace Church. Grace's vision is to help everyone become an outward-focused follower of Jesus. Grace has three locations in Kansas City (two in Overland Park and one in Olathe) and is committed to training and sending 100 church planters and missionaries over 20 years. Tim graduated from Stanford University with a degree in Computer Systems Engineering and worked at Black & Veatch as an engineer while being trained for ministry. Tim is the creator of three OWNit365 Bible reading plans to help make Bible reading simple, understandable, and applicable to your daily life. Tim is the author of two books: a discipleship book called *Love Jesus* and a Bible-in-a-year devotional called *One Story: Encountering Jesus through the Bible*. Tim and his wife Cathy met at Stanford and have three children: Jacob, Karina, and Mallon. They currently reside in Overland Park, Kansas.

Made in the USA
Columbia, SC
31 December 2021

52973603R10205